I0709634

A
SOUTHERN
VERSE

PETER STITT

Daylight

Cofounders: Taj Forer and Michael Itkoff
Creative Director: Ursula Damm
Copy Editor: Gabrielle Fastman

ISBN: 978-1-942084-94-5

Printed by Ofset Yapimevi, Turkey

Daylight Books
E-mail: info@daylightbooks.org
Web: www.daylightbooks.org

INTRODUCTION

Augusta, Georgia, is a big small town, somewhat quizzically the second largest city in the state of Georgia, and frequently confused about its standing. And while the city may be seated in the state of Georgia, it more accurately resides in Georgia-lina, a scrappy amalgamation of Georgia and South Carolina, or more specifically, the borders of those two states. Below the fall line, sandy and full of pine trees, the types of places surrounding Augusta, Georgia, are spotted with convenience stores, churches, schools, and Dollar Generals.

I first got to know Pete at the Soul Bar, an Augusta institution dedicated to another Augusta institution, the R&B legend James Brown. The Soul Bar is one of those picture-perfect dive bars held together with expired show flyers, masking tape, and funky ephemera reflective of its patrons and proprietors—things just live there. When it opened in the fall of 1995, the Soul Bar, along with a few other like-minded businesses, was creating a new downtown in place of one that had largely been abandoned for suburbs and malls—conditions not unique to Augusta. After a few years of successfully hosting dance parties at various places around town, the Soul Bar's founders were able to open a spot of their own when, in an effort to incentivize investment in the struggling downtown, the city made loans available to enterprising individuals in hopes that new energy could help revive the central business district.

Soul Bar's real spirit is a little bit scrappy, a little bohemian, and very supportive of a close-knit community of artists and musicians. It isn't a coincidence that Pete was there; he seemed to know most everyone and could carry on at length with just about anyone, about anything. I'm not sure if it was the unmistakable colors of the Kodak tattoo on Pete's arm that provided an entry into one of our early conversations about photography, but I remember feeling very surprised that we shared a mutual appreciation for a very similar kind of work. Our enthusiasm for the quirky photographs of William Eggleston was one of the first of many points of conversation about photography and I relished an understanding and comfort in talking to someone who enjoyed some of the same things I did and seemed to enjoy them with a similar passion. Finding an ally in Pete, I would give him details of upcoming shows and lectures at the local art museum I worked at.

At the time, I knew nothing of his work and was perfectly content just to talk about other photographers and gear. I pretended to dabble, but truthfully, even referring to myself as a hobbyist would be generous. I envied Pete's Leica and even sheepishly asked him if he could take a headshot I needed for an upcoming DJ gig. I don't think he had the heart to tell me he wasn't that kind of photographer, and we both pretended to be "that thing" as he took my picture. We talked about his schooling, time spent at Northeastern University studying photography, an unlucky stretch at the Savannah College of Art and Design, studio assistant work, and the desire to make art.

Pete's father had grown a successful business in supplying portable toilets, and Pete found himself working to provide toilets to job sites and events; the serviceable area was large, and portables can go just about anywhere. Pete's time was split between the company office and trips to those "just about anywhere" places. It's here I like to imagine that the seeds for this book started, driving through New Ellenton or Gaston—unlikely places for contemporary "Art Photography"—delivering toilets.

In a leap of faith, Pete opened a gallery on the 1100 block of Broad Street in downtown Augusta. Billed as Artists Local 1155, the gallery was important, although I don't know if anyone had the foresight to say so at the time. Existing for three short years, the place, like so many other artist-run spaces, was a labor of love. Keeping hours complementary to the nightlife that surrounded it, the gallery came alive on weekend evenings and seemed to cater to people unlikely to visit more traditional spaces. Work was priced incredibly low, and there was a sense that anyone could get a show if they had the nerve to approach Pete with an idea. During its run it hosted student exhibitions and ragamuffin group shows, and occasionally, if you were lucky, or if someone's plans fell through last minute, selections of Pete's large color prints flanking both sides of its narrow walls.

I think it was around this time that it became clear Pete was working toward something. His pictures belonged together, and there were early signs that he was processing a body of work. New images added to the growing language that was developing. A creature of habit, Pete would seek out his subjects in the small towns surrounding his home in North Augusta, South Carolina. The humor may be lost in writing it, but I like to imagine Pete pulling into a small town like Johnston, South Carolina, in his then-characteristic Mini Cooper, to photograph a parking lot. If you hang around photographers enough, these juxtapositions of artists in the wild seem less rare. However, rarer still is the fact that this is happening at all in places like Modoc or Saluda.

Eventually, I convinced Pete to help with a digital photography camp we offered to teenagers at the museum. Through a generous gift from Nikon by way of a retired local sports photographer, we suddenly had a cache of inexpensive cameras. Over the course of a couple of years, we spent weeks each summer teaching students about basic technical aspects of photography while wandering around, shooting pictures, and extolling the virtues of street photography and anything else we thought might keep their attention. A quiet force amongst the students, Pete approached teaching the way I assume he approaches his picture-making, with a loose plan and an open mind as to what might be uncovered through work. We walked and looked, and gave students the opportunity to do the same.

A highlight of each week was seeing the photographs Pete took. Despite returning to the same locations, there always seemed to be a fresh inspiration and views the rest of us missed.

A lot has changed in photography since William Eggleston first exhibited his then-controversial color photographs in 1969. Another respected Southern photographer at the time, Walker Evans, echoed the sentiment of much of the old guard, and a potentially hesitant artworld, summarizing his feelings squarely: "There are four simple words for the matter, which must be whispered: color photography is vulgar." This attitude was in no doubt relative to the light in which color photography had been previously cast; relegated to advertising and commercial work, I can imagine that the emergence of color art photography might have seemed crass, and in the case of Eggleston, even the subject matter reflected a sensibility that seemed fixated on the mundane, with signage, suburban sprawl, and shopping carts filling the frame.

Pete's work continues much of this tradition, a window into the very specifics of a place captured with unexpected vitality. The "idea" of a place is tricky; to coalesce the experience or the identity requires a kind of editing that is hard to pinpoint. I often wonder how these images might read seen from afar and removed from their environment. These works don't contain the obvious. Could an intriguing contemporary landscape be seen in a sign for a "Wal-Mart Coming Soon?" Could the humor of cross-generational noise in a small town be translated? Can the mundane and the beautiful coexist, and what exactly are we doing here? To look at this collection, we are riding shotgun with Pete and encouraged to marvel at a landscape that is often humorous, bleak, and frequently without answers. A doorway entrance blocked by the removable bench seating of a van; a makeshift composition of unlikely components, like the once-festive frayed bunting celebrating the space underneath a window air-conditioning unit in *A/C Flags, North, SC*, or elsewhere with a tank frozen in memorial, casting a shadow, somewhat ominously framing a quaint house in the background. In *Headstones, Neeces, SC*, a display of grave markers is interrupted by the advertising sign of the man who has made them. The result seems to suggest a humorous allegory of the ultimate balancing act—between work and life, and life and death. In another image, these forces appear quietly; in *Red Solo Cup, Joanna, SC*, we see a lone Solo cup, tipped sideways, discarded on the ground, a modern vanitas spilled across a parking lot.

The reception of these photographs beyond Georgia-lina and among a broader public seems encouraging, as is the inclusion of recent photographs in shows as far afield as Vienna, Paris, and Budapest. There's much to enjoy here, most of which is a unique vision about a place often misunderstood, and the emerging voice that has so deftly captured it.

—Matt Porter

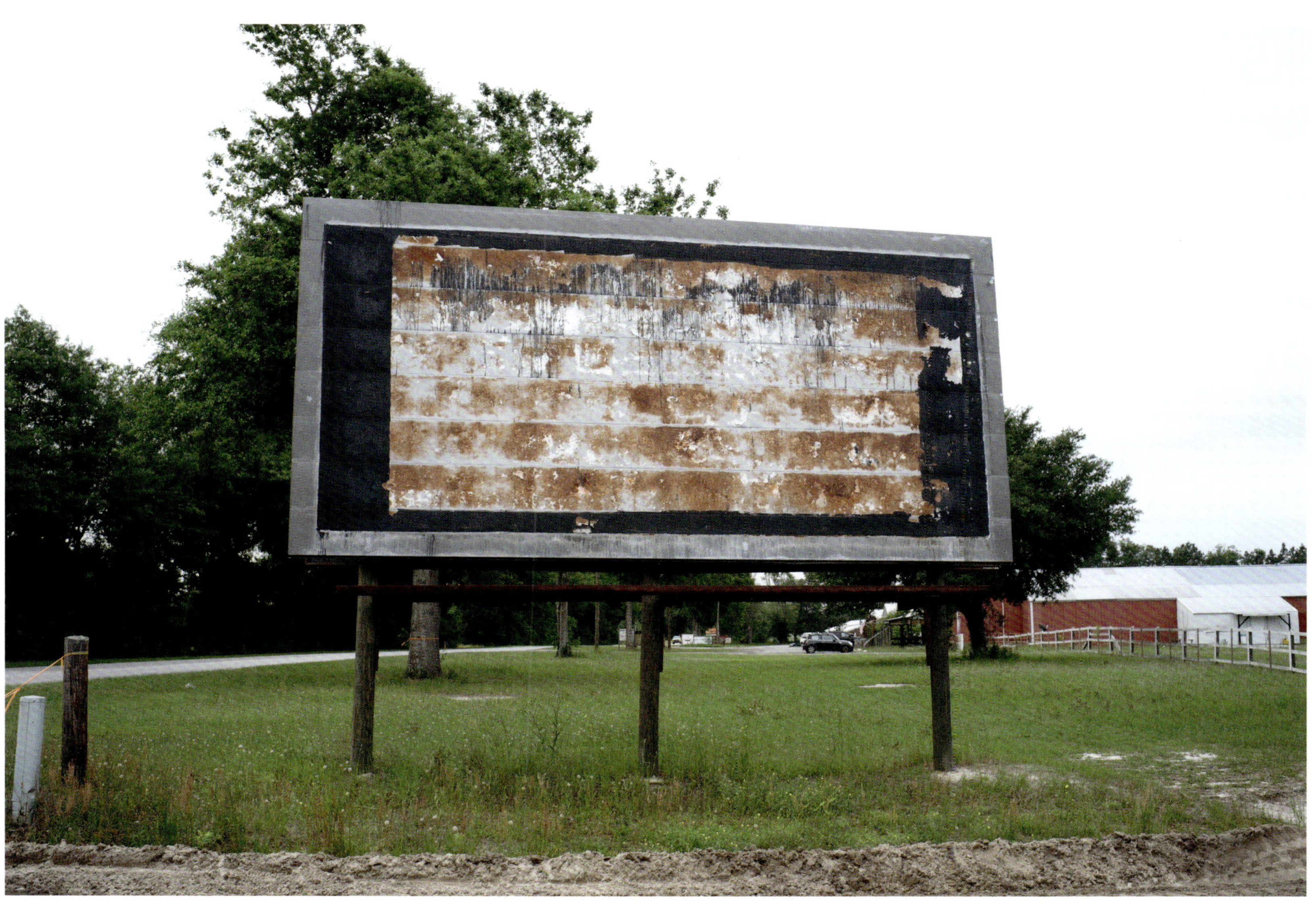

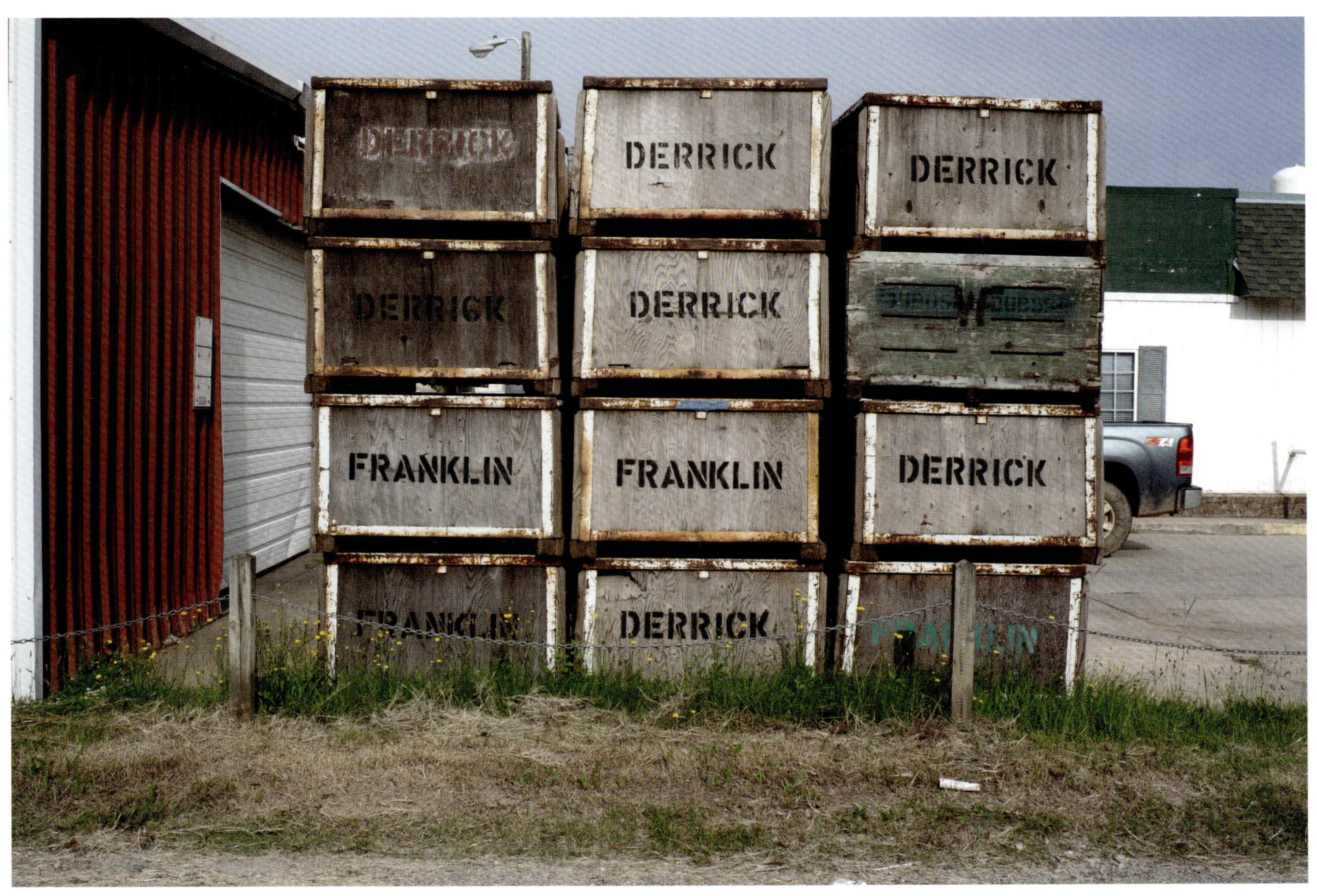

DERRICK
DERRICK
DERRICK
DERRICK
DERRICK
DERRICK
FRANKLIN
FRANKLIN
DERRICK
FRANKLIN
DERRICK
FRANKLIN

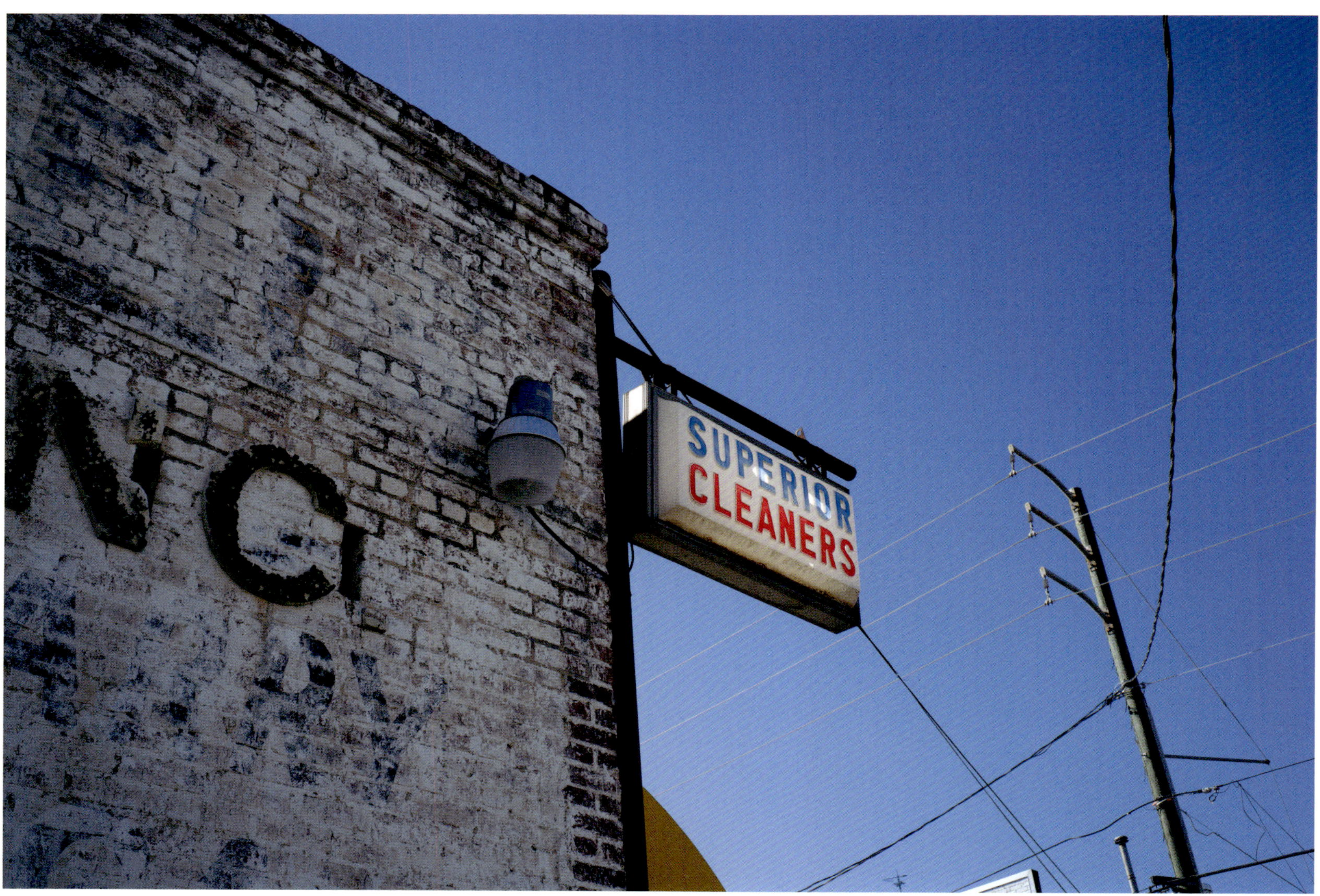
SUPERIOR
CLEANERS

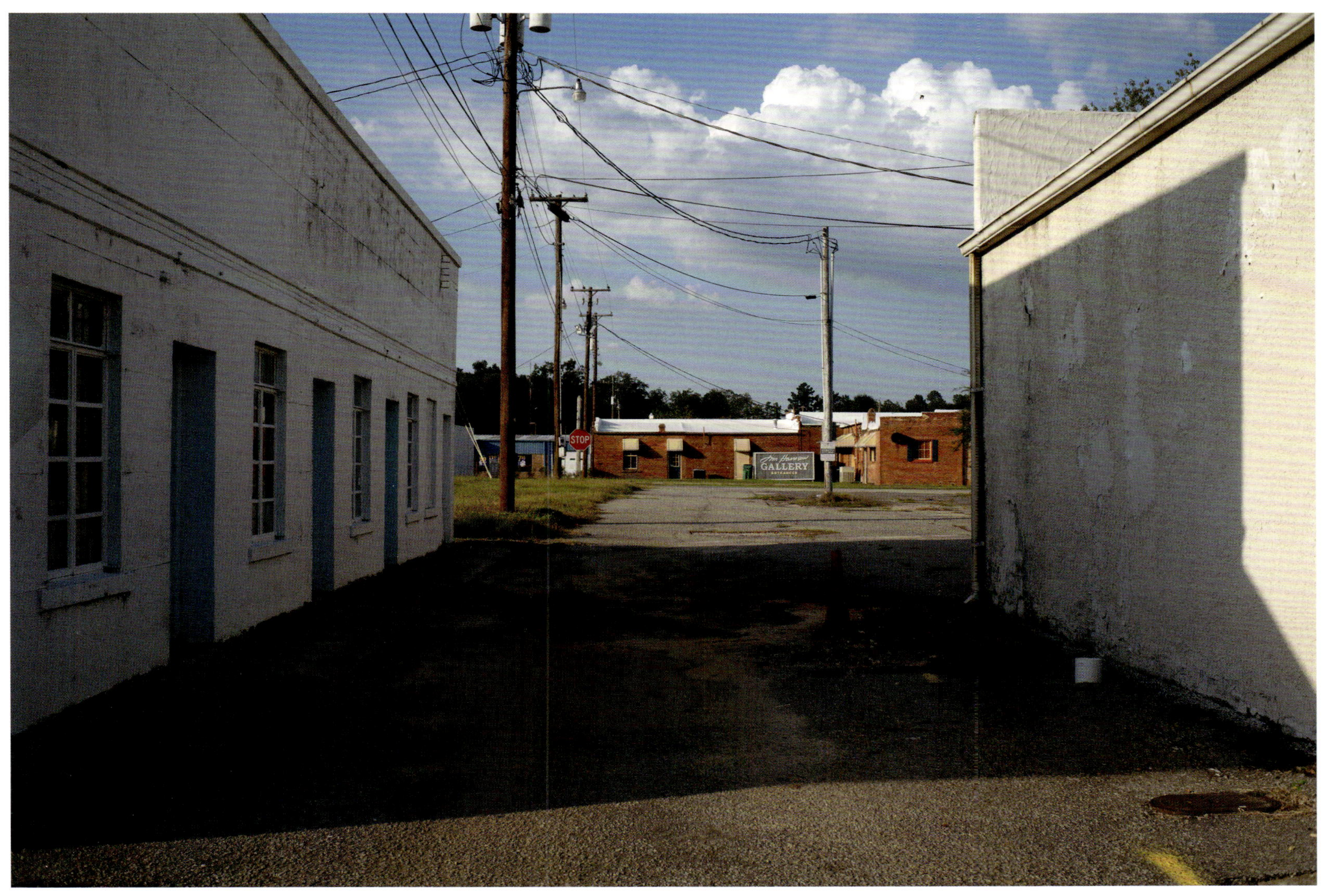

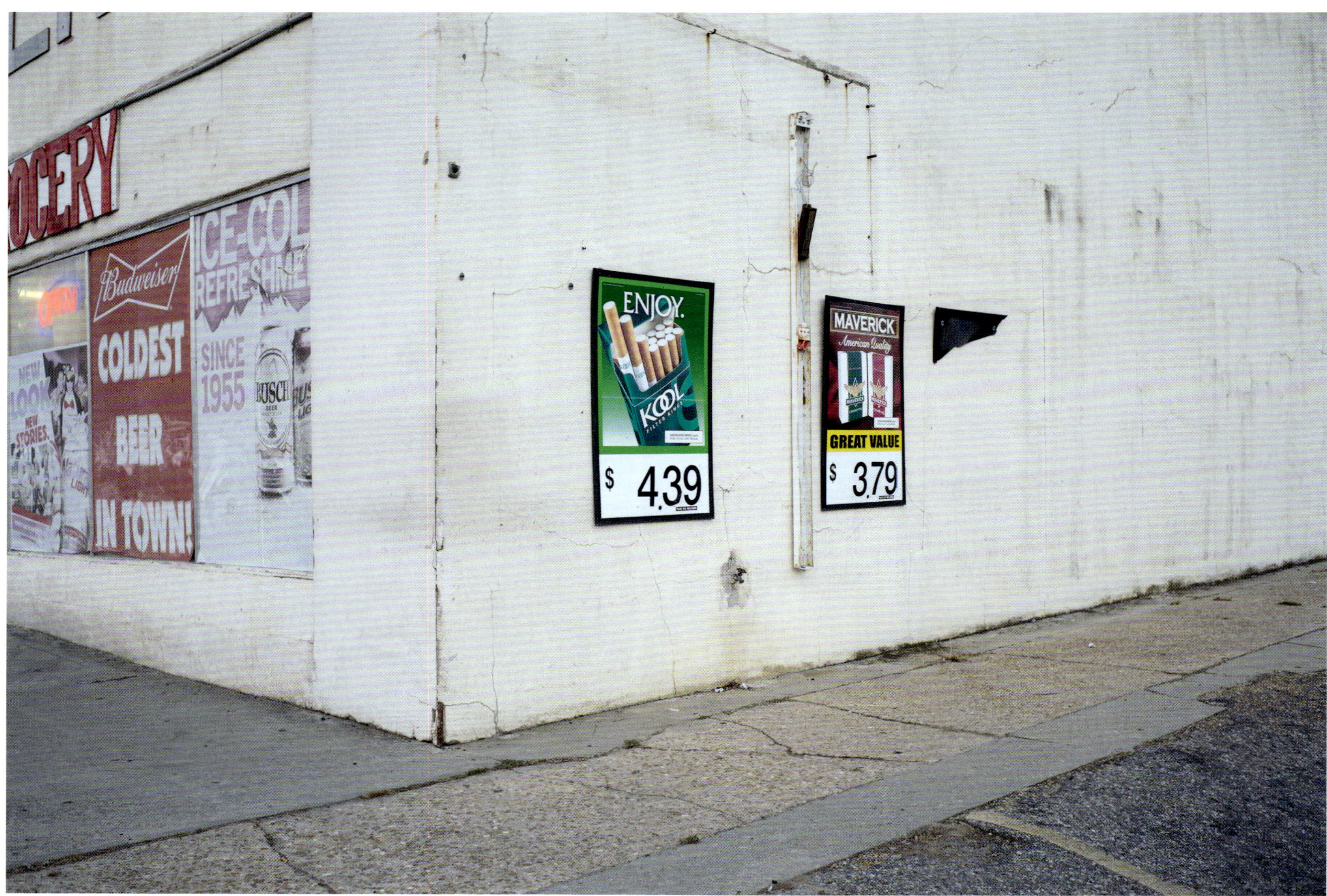
GROCERY
Budweiser!
ICE-COL
REFRESHME
COLDEST
BEER
IN TOWN!
SINCE
1955
BUSCH
BEER
NEW
LOOK
NEW
STORIES
ENJOY.
KOOL
FILTER KING
$ 4.39
MAVERICK
American Quality
GREAT VALUE
$ 3.79

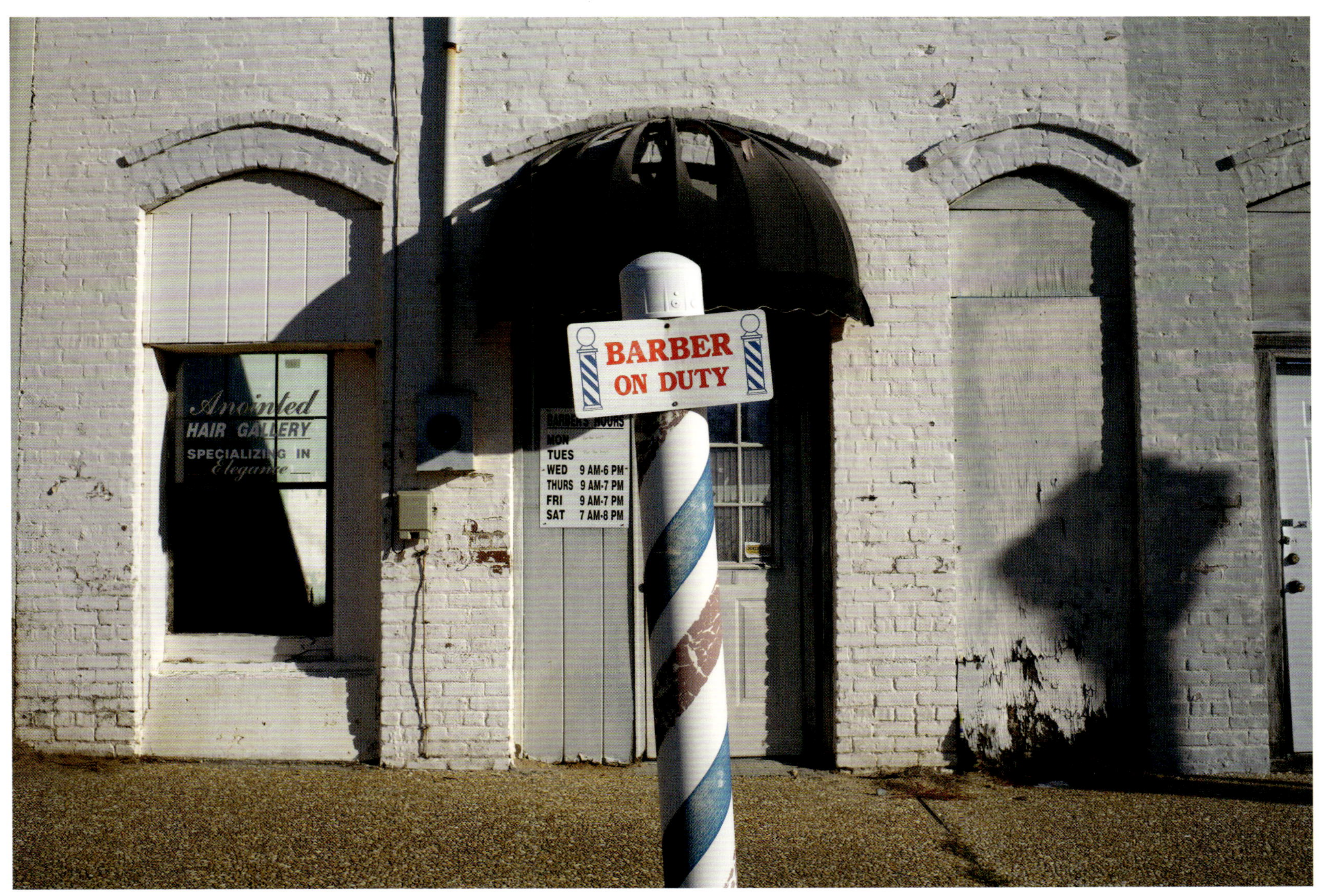
Anointed
HAIR GALLERY
SPECIALIZING IN
Elegance
BARBER
ON DUTY
BARBER HOURS
MON
TUES
WED   9 AM-6 PM
THURS   9 AM-7 PM
FRI   9 AM-7 PM
SAT   7 AM-8 PM

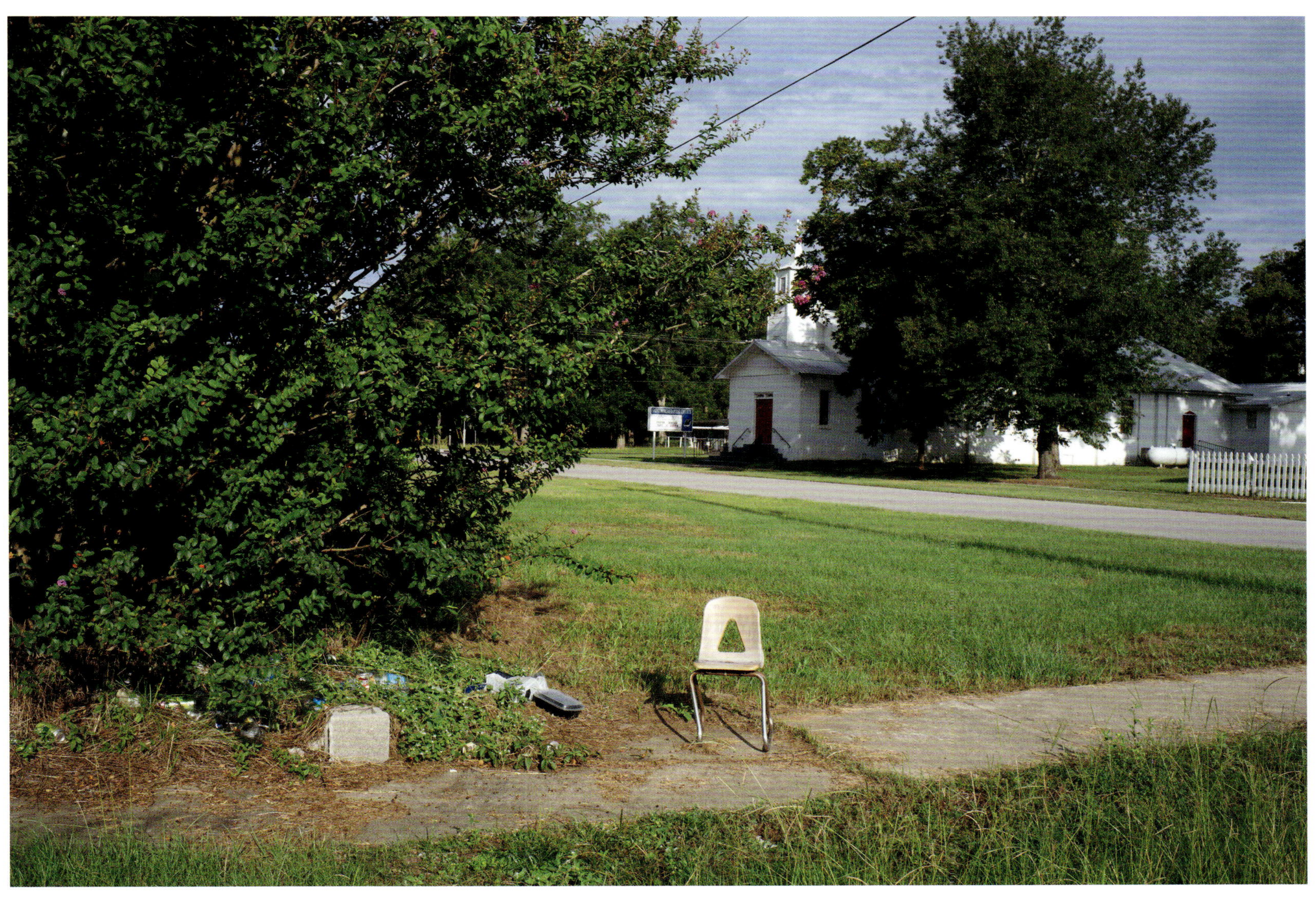

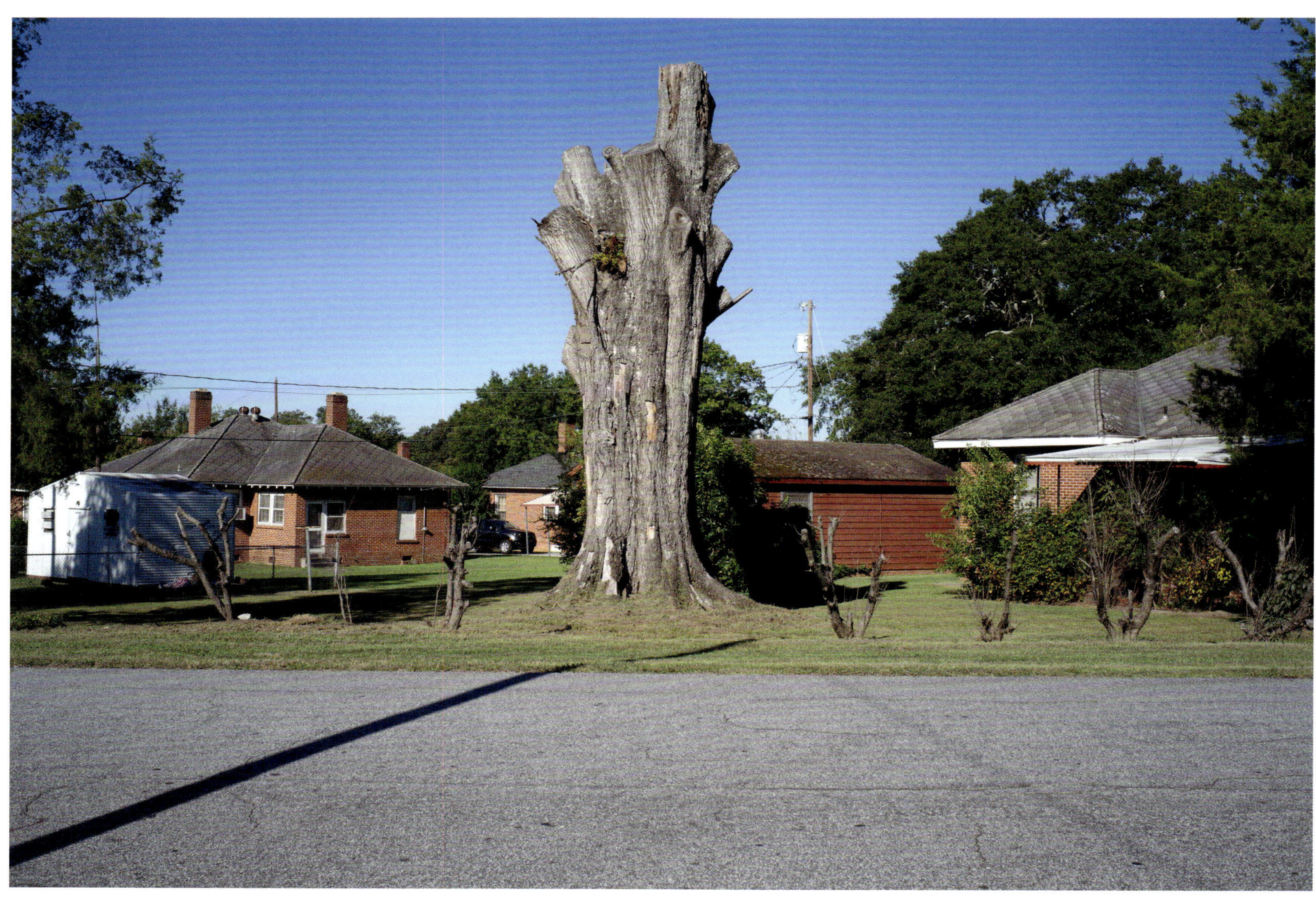

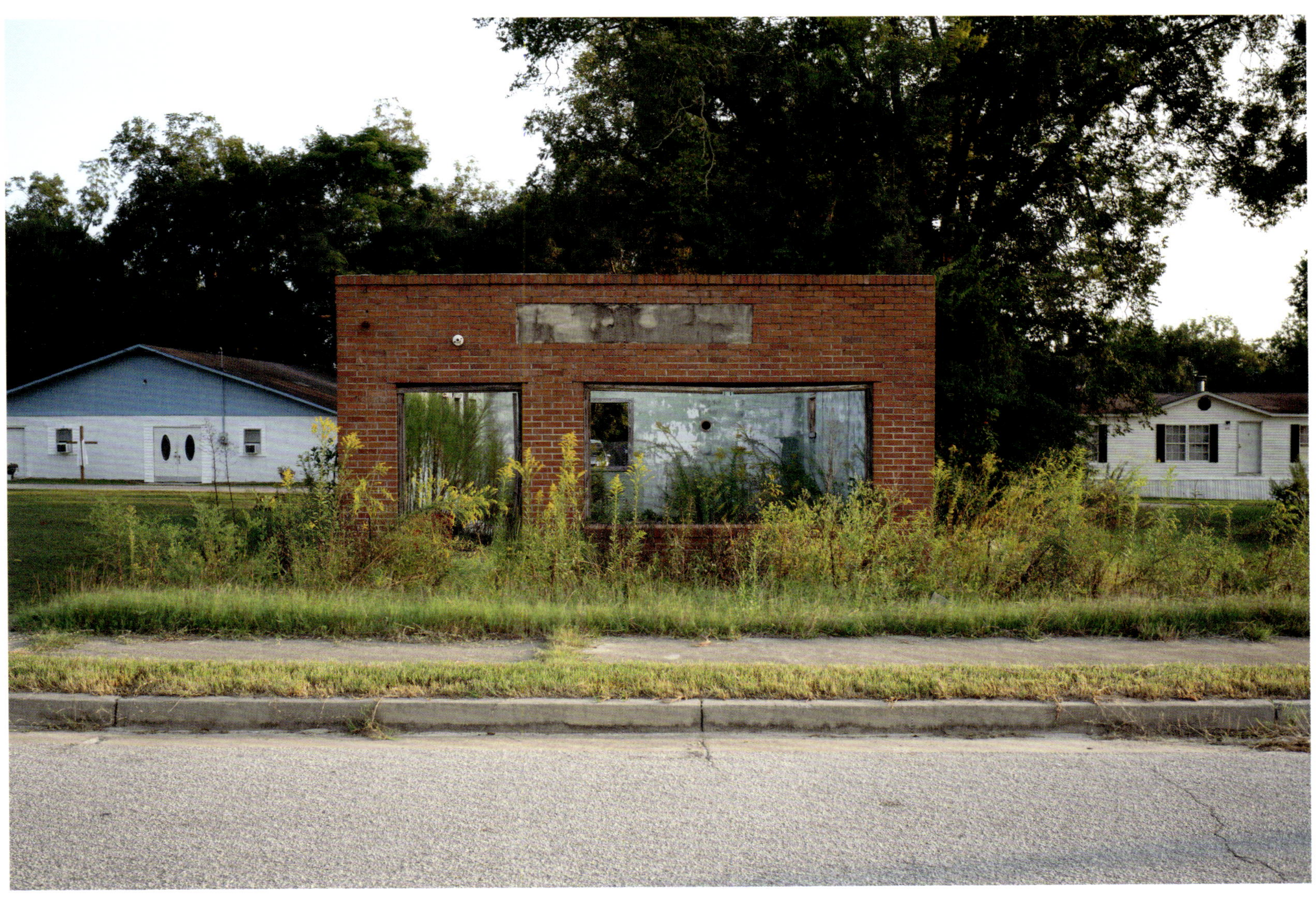

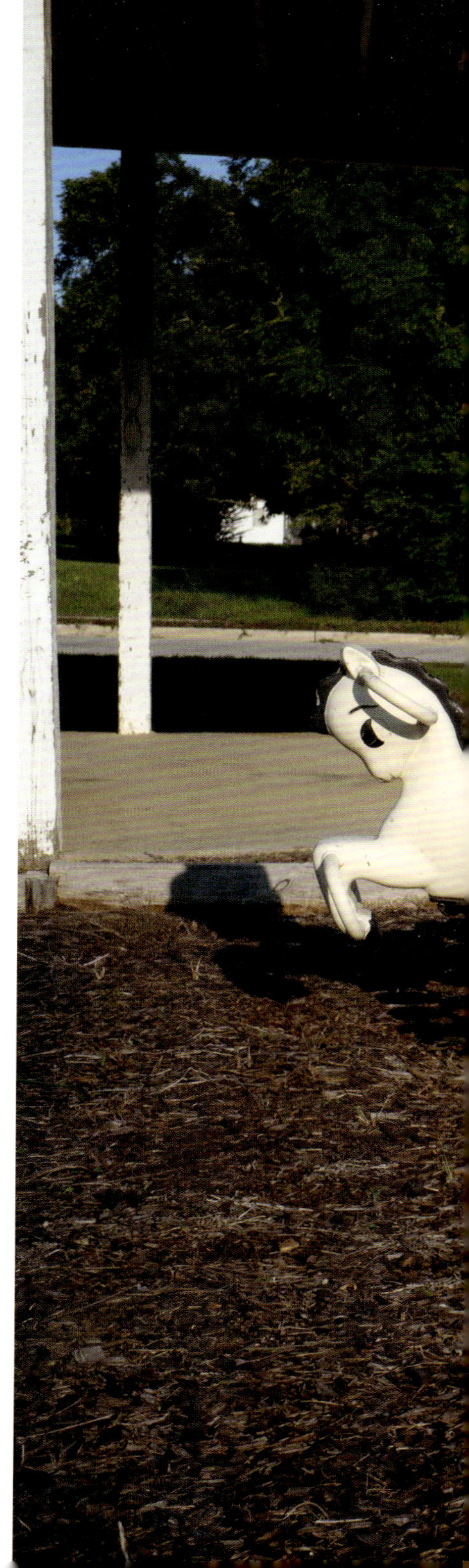

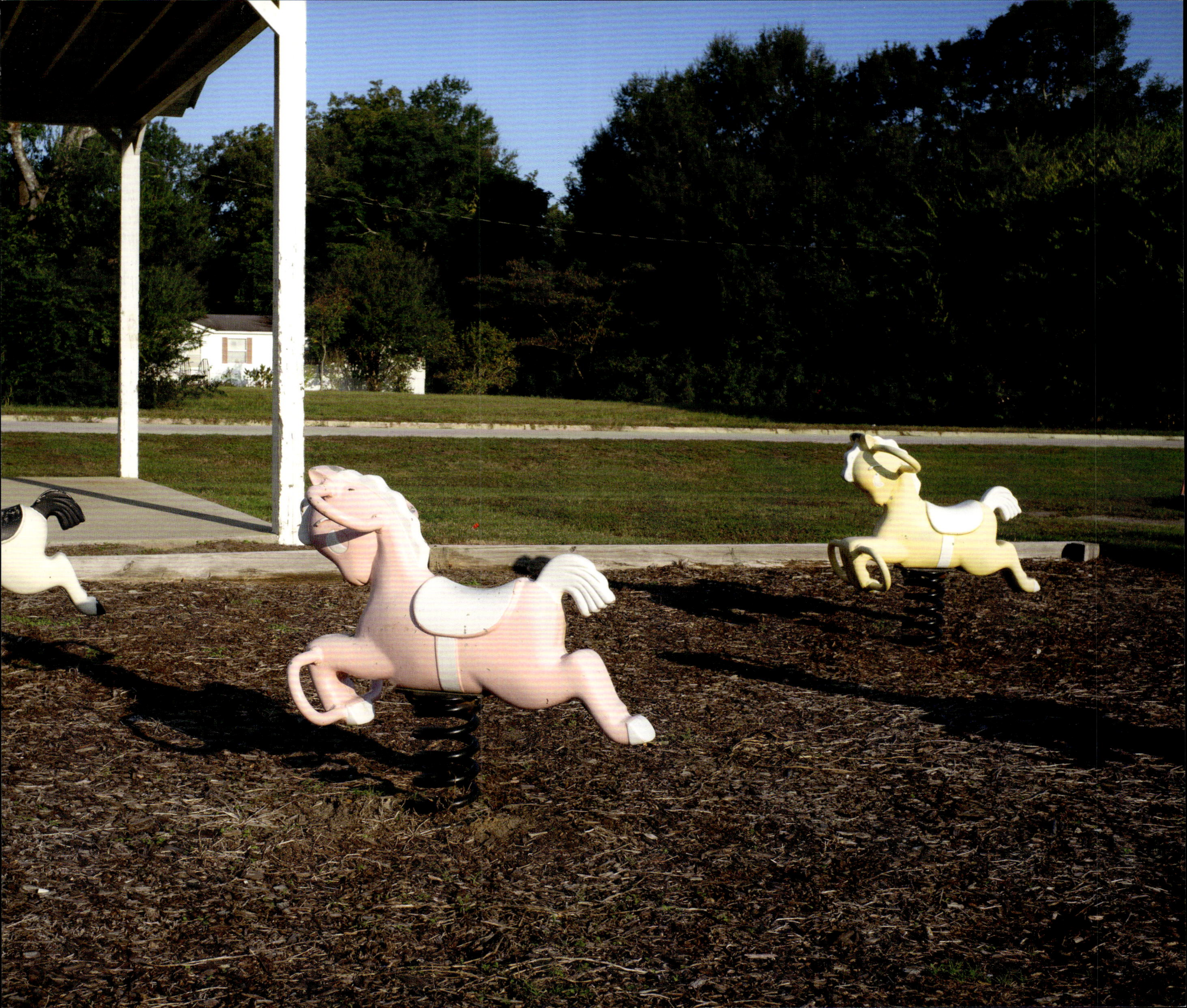

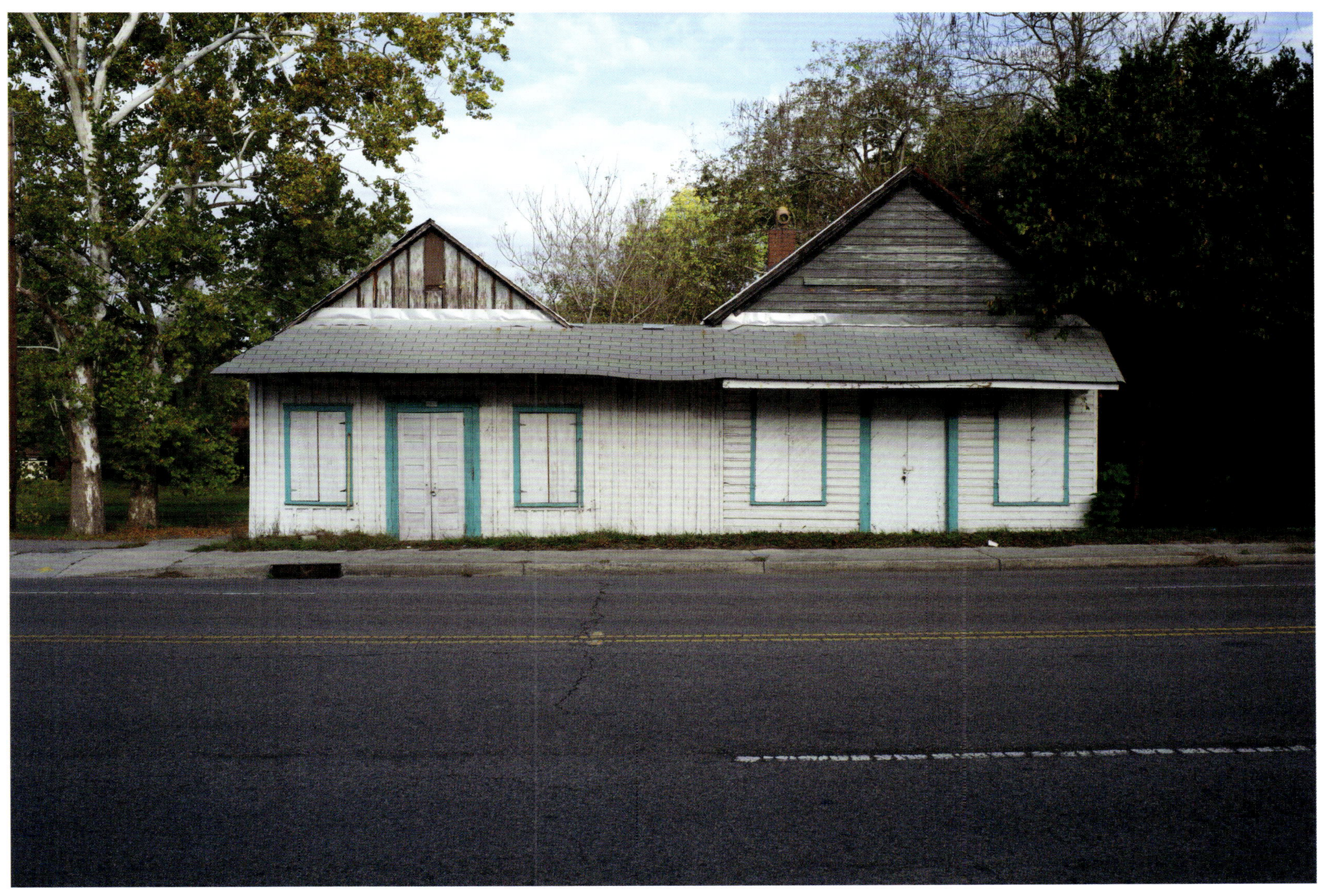

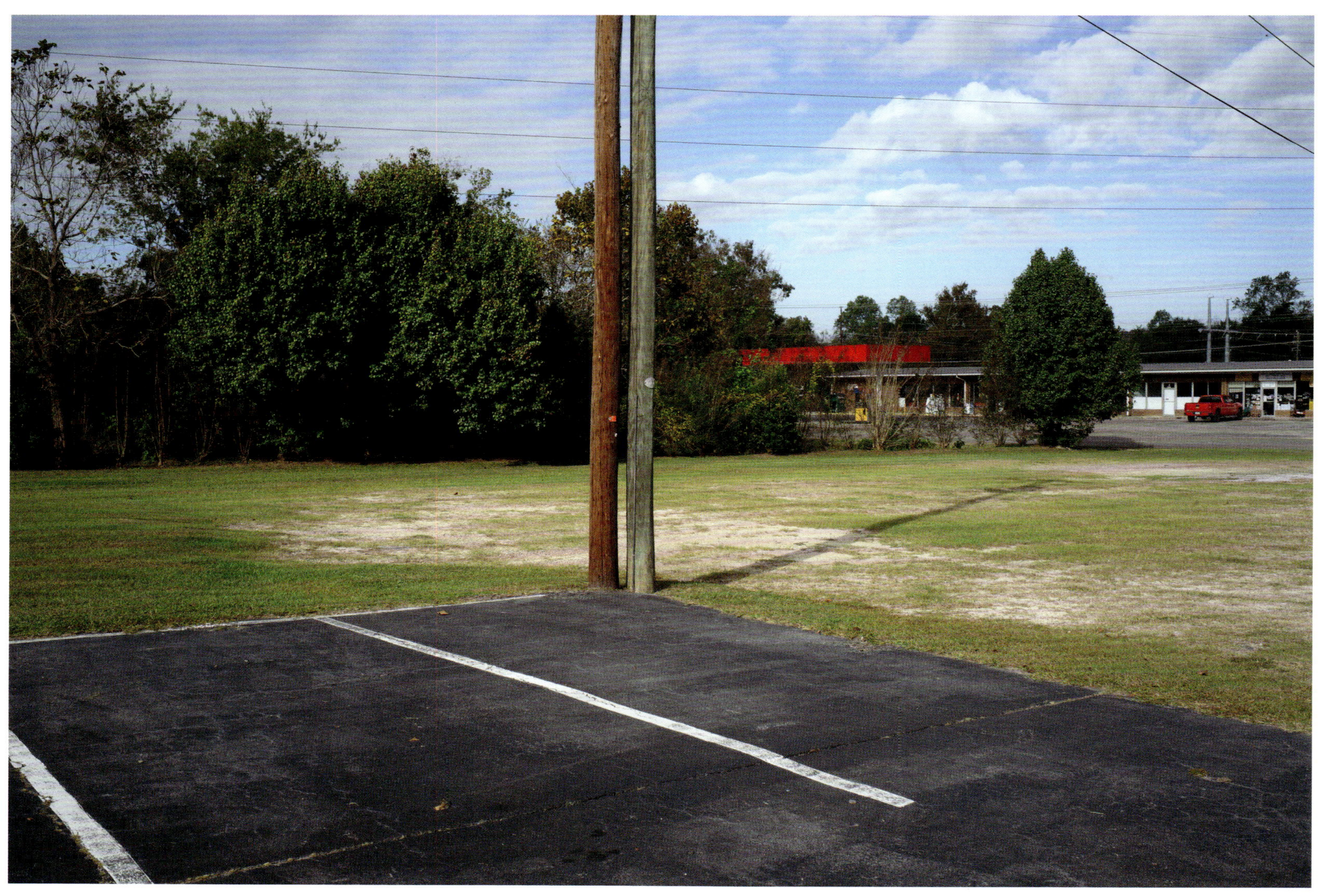

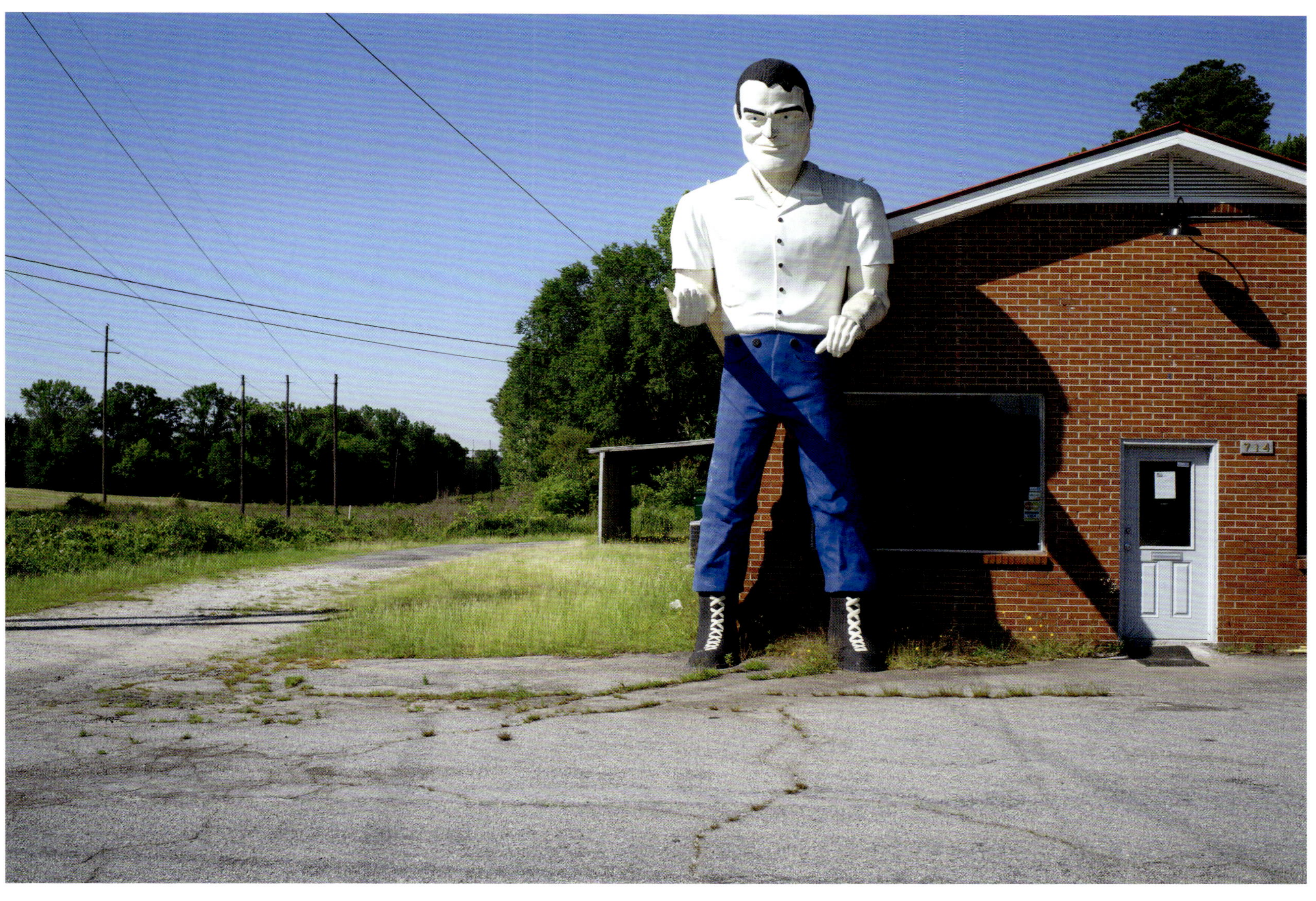

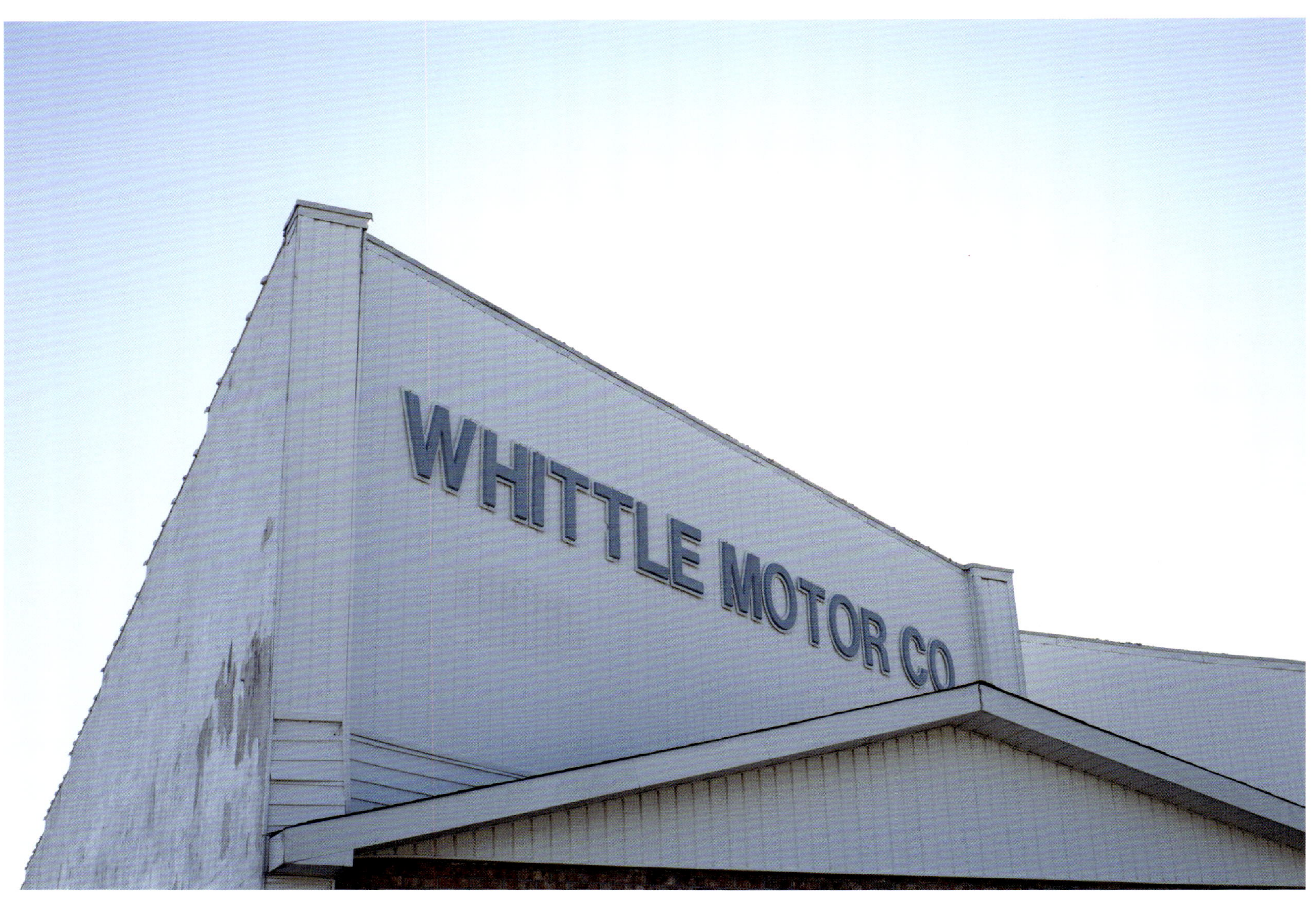

WHITTLE MOTOR CO

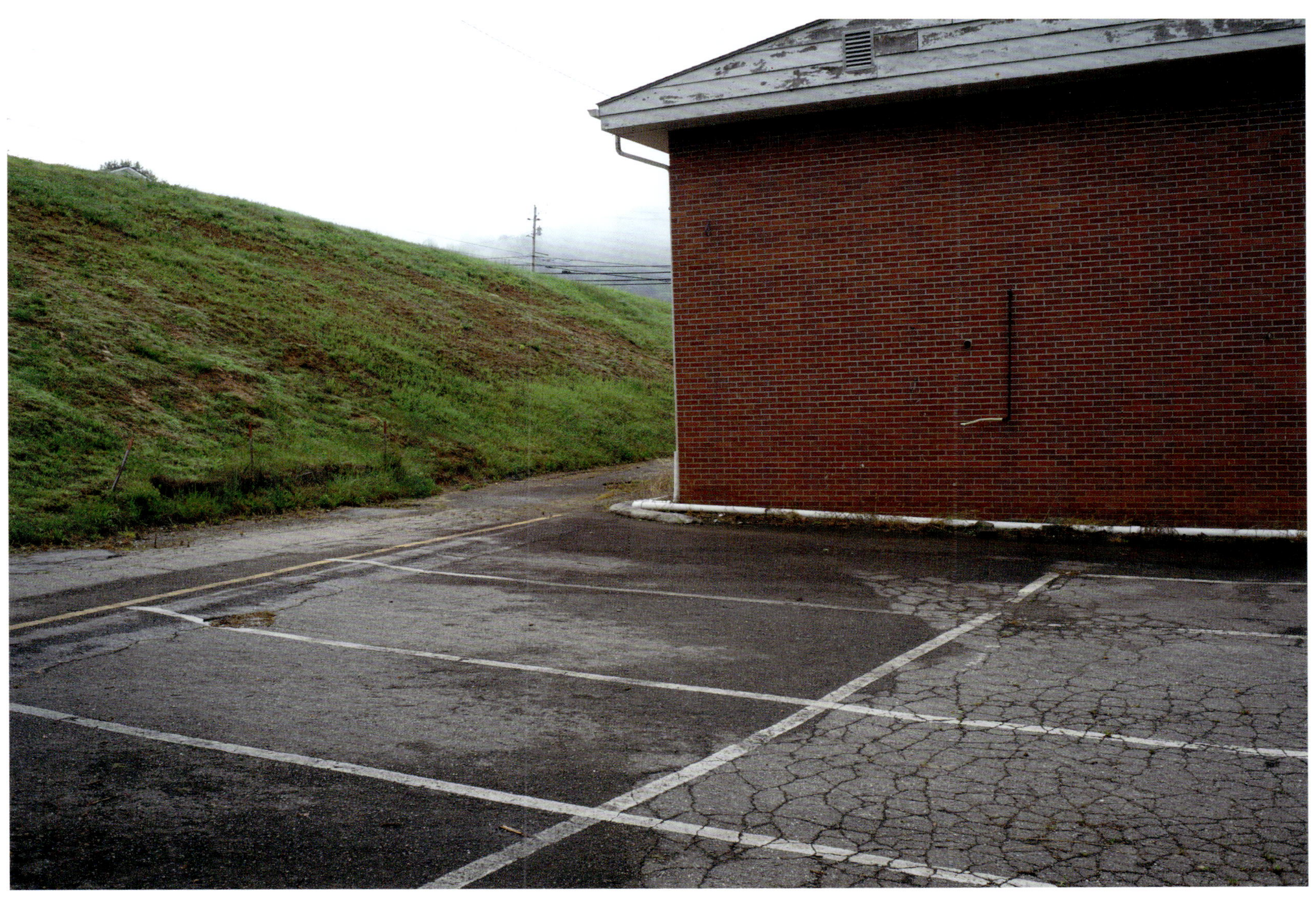

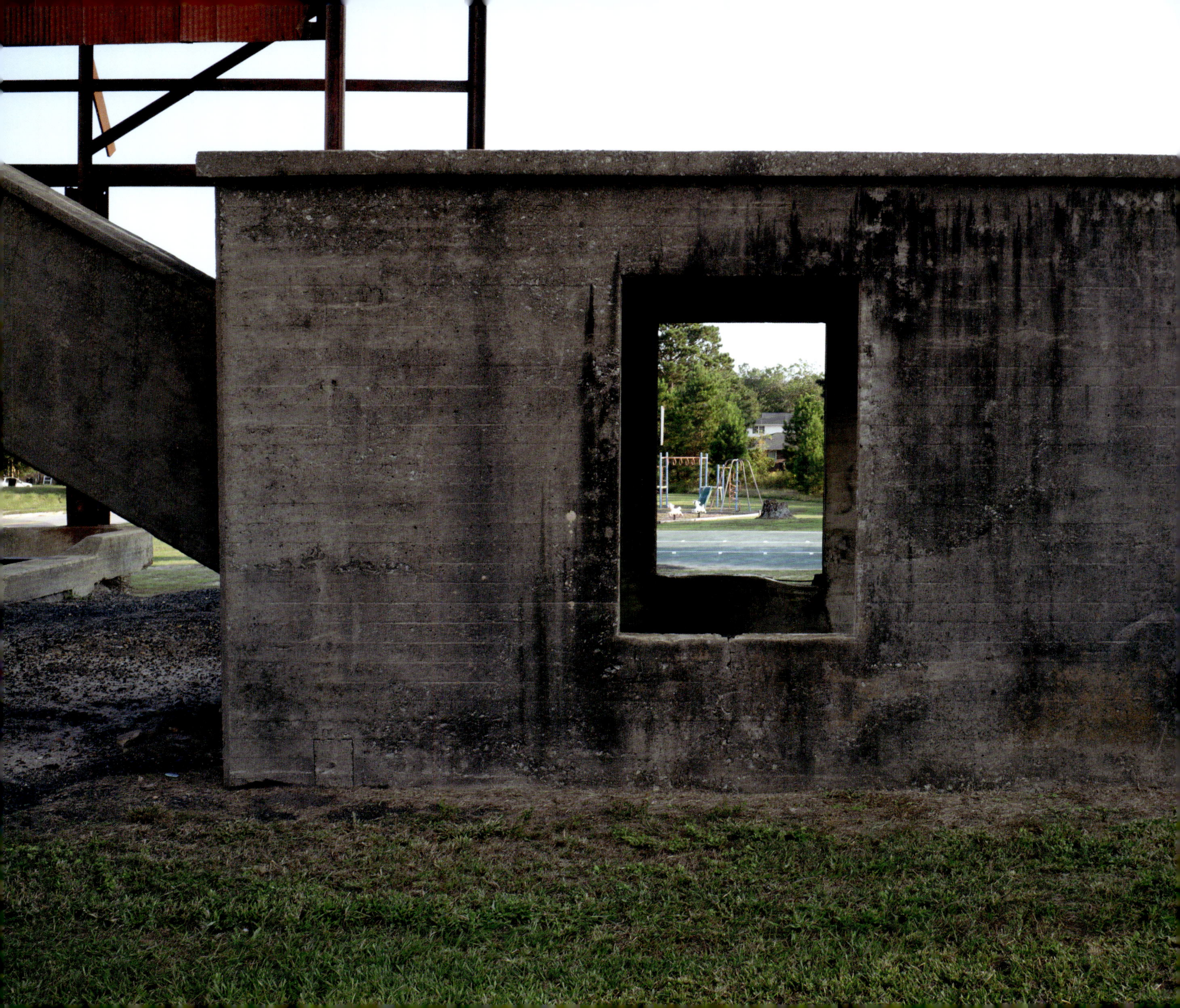

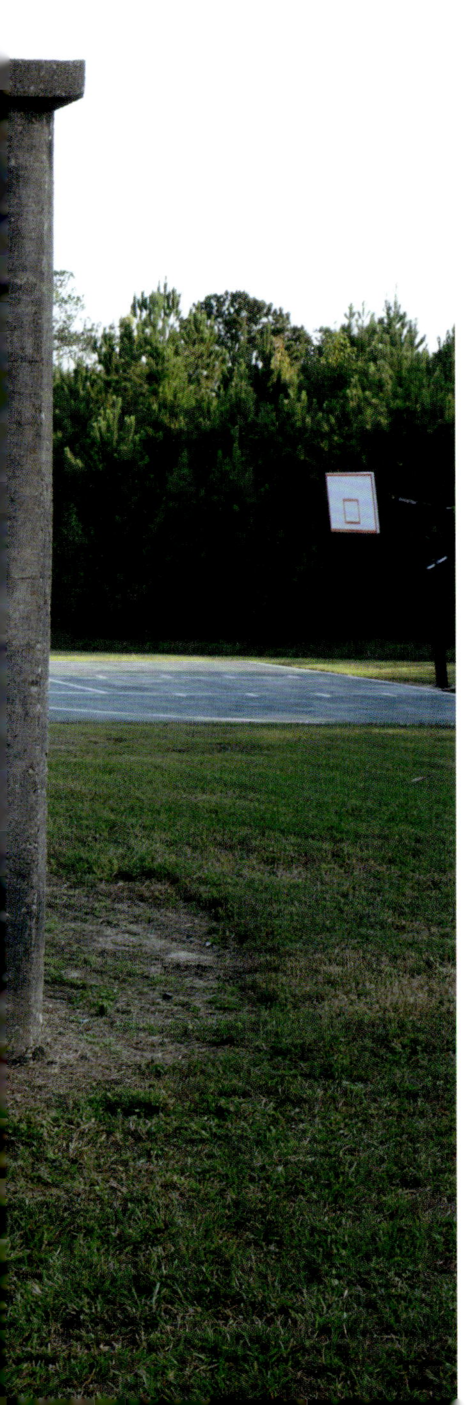

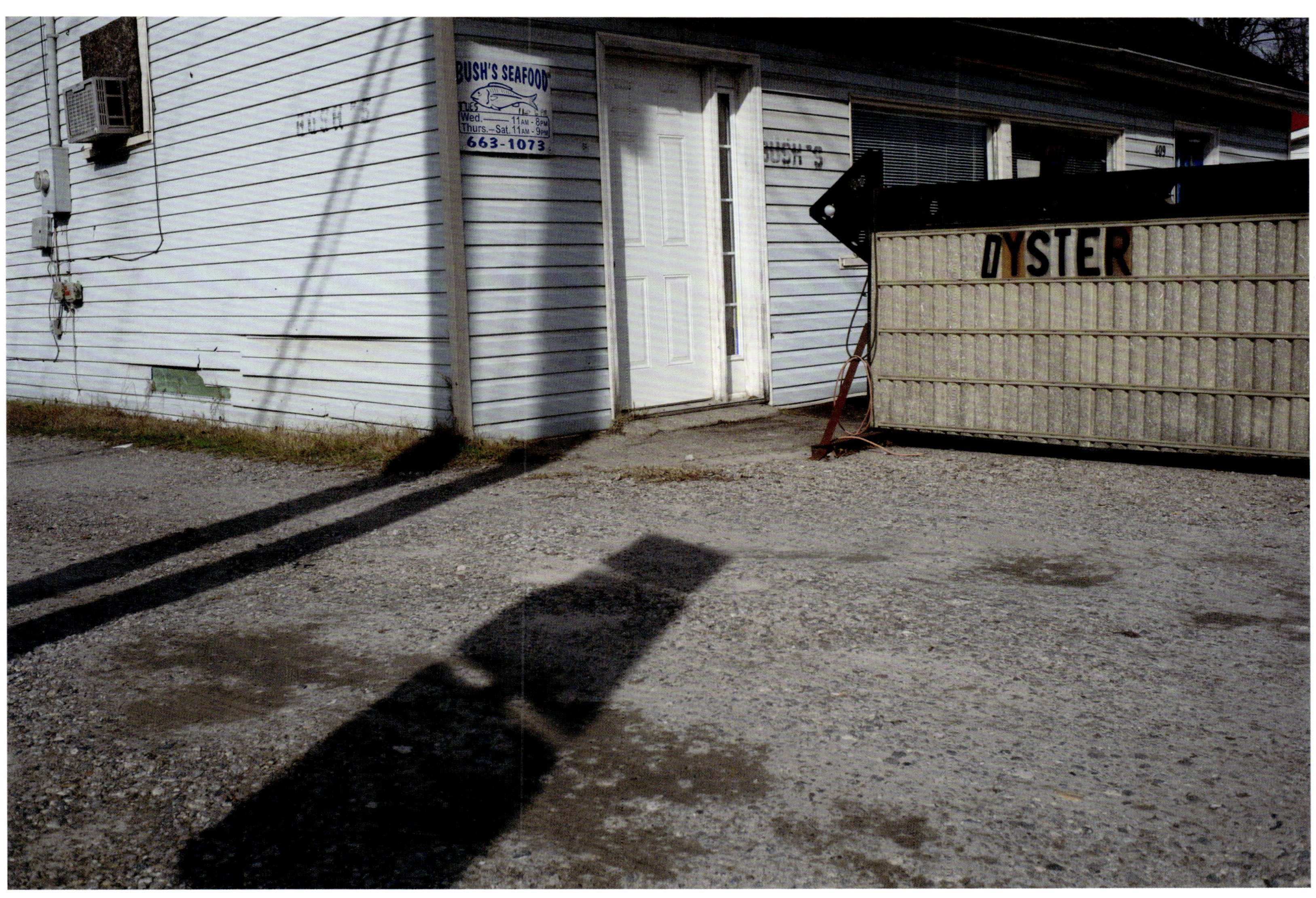
BUSH'S SEAFOOD
Tues. 11AM–8PM
Wed. 11AM–8PM
Thurs.–Sat. 11AM–9PM
663-1073
BUSH'S
409
OYSTER

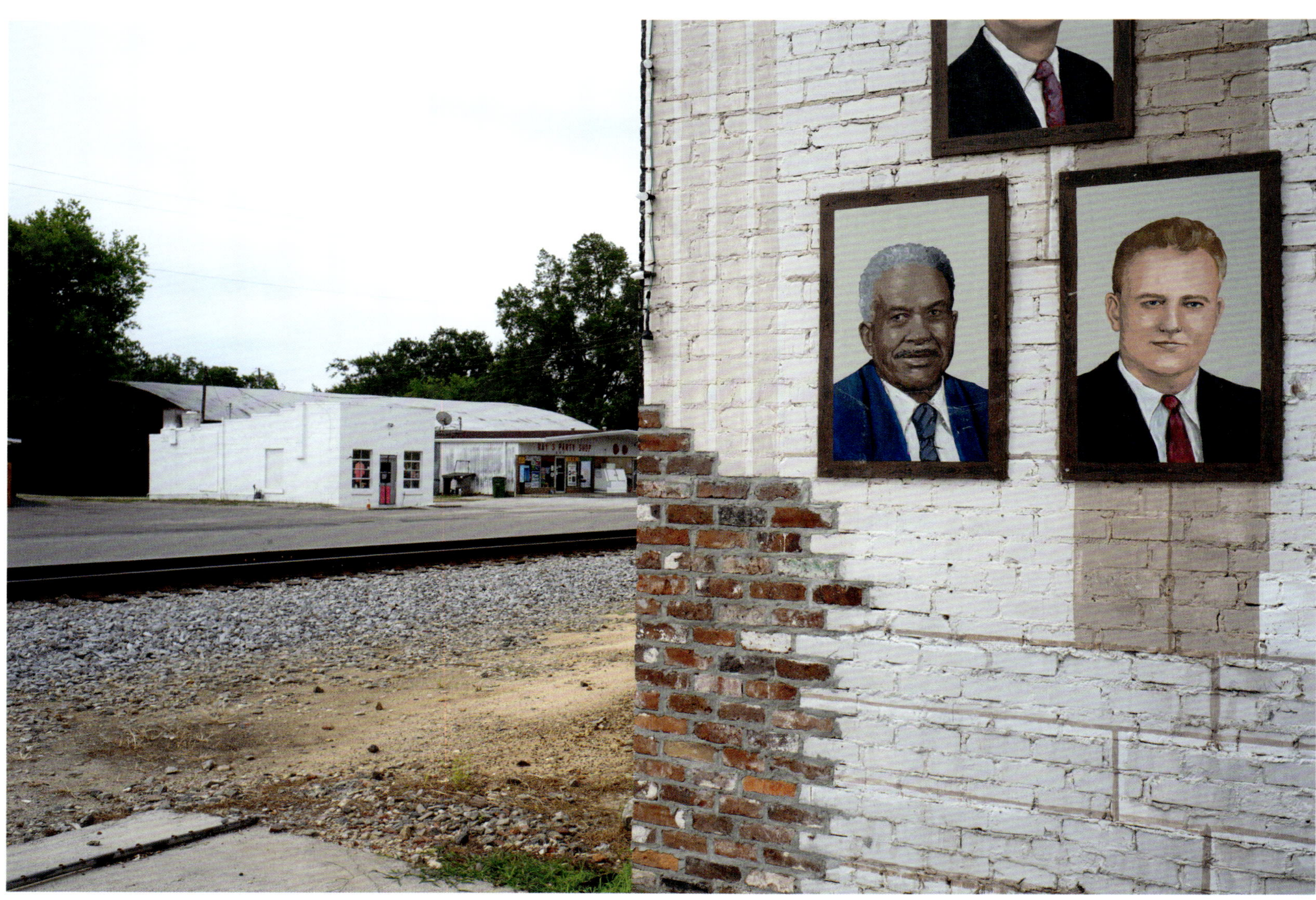

RAY'S PARTY SHOP

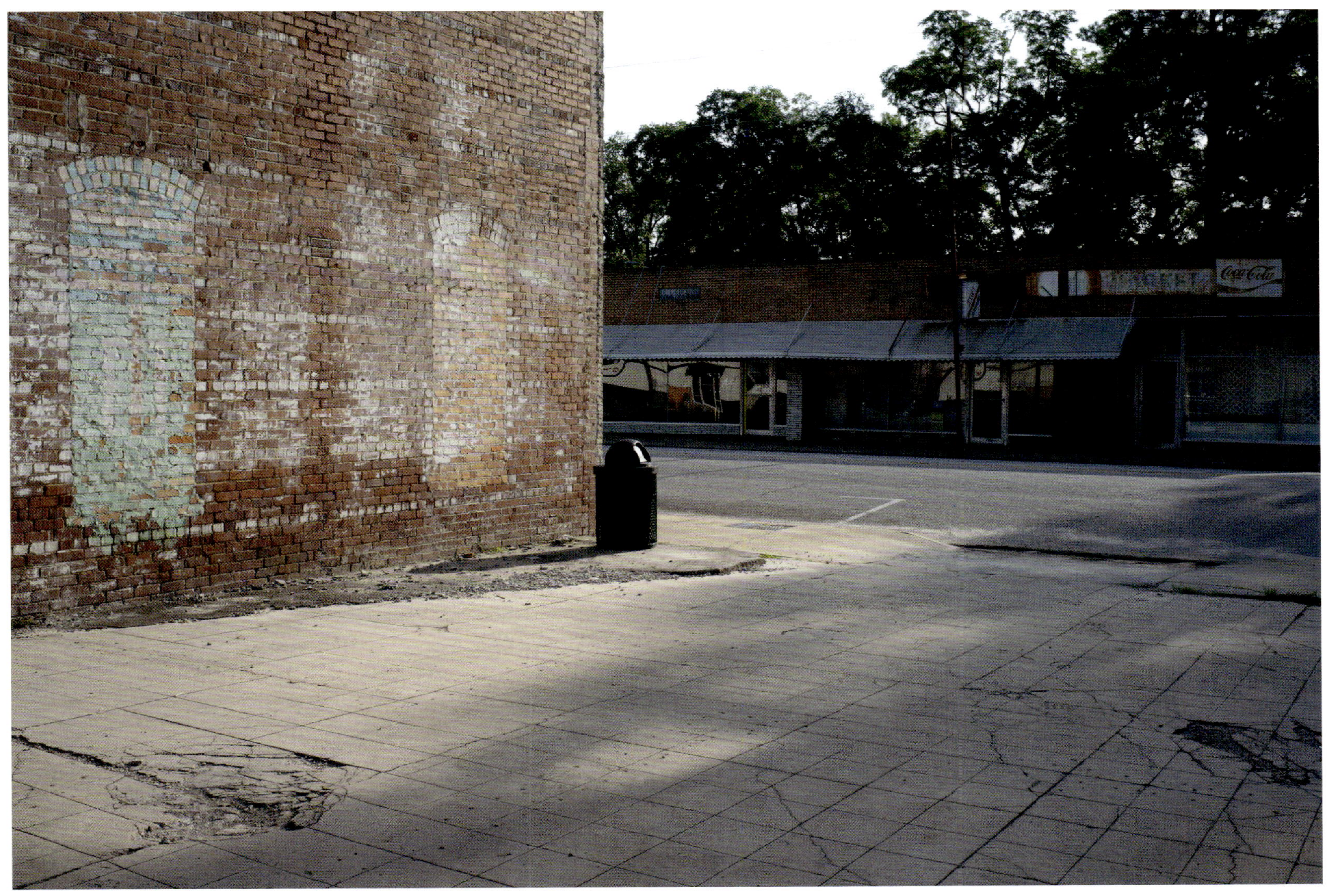

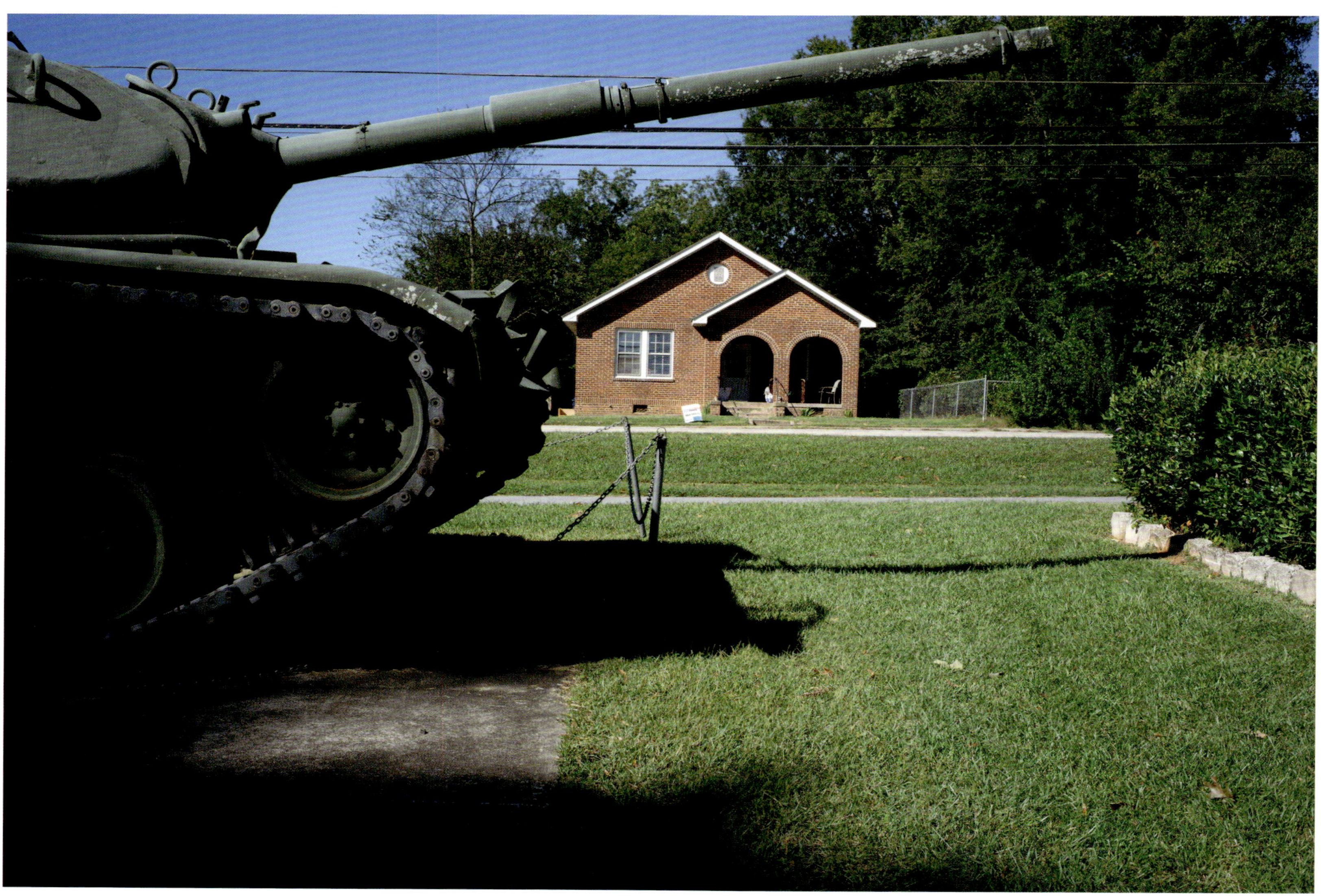

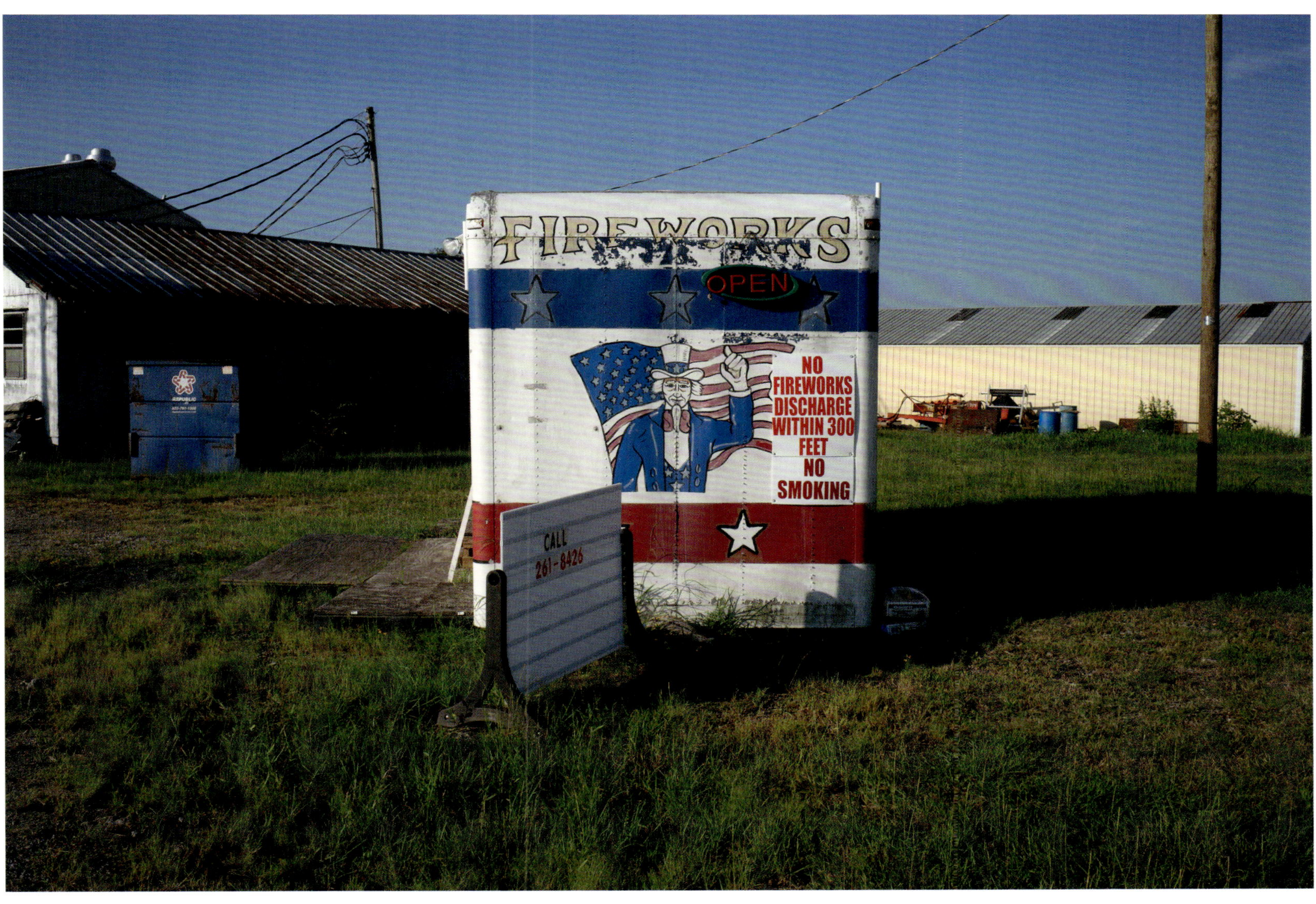
FIREWORKS
OPEN
NO
FIREWORKS
DISCHARGE
WITHIN 300
FEET
NO
SMOKING
CALL
261-8426

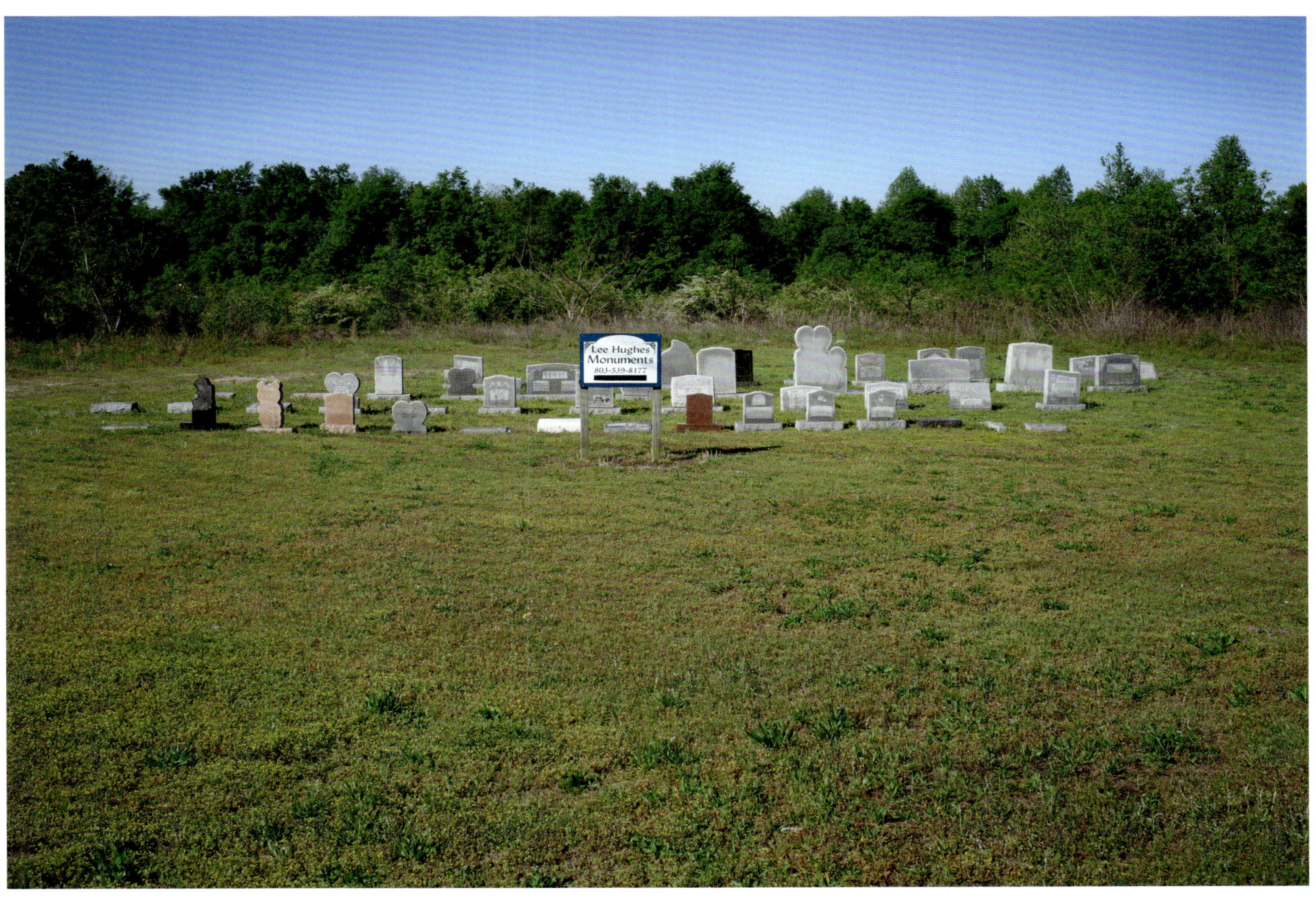

Lee Hughes
Monuments
803-539-8177

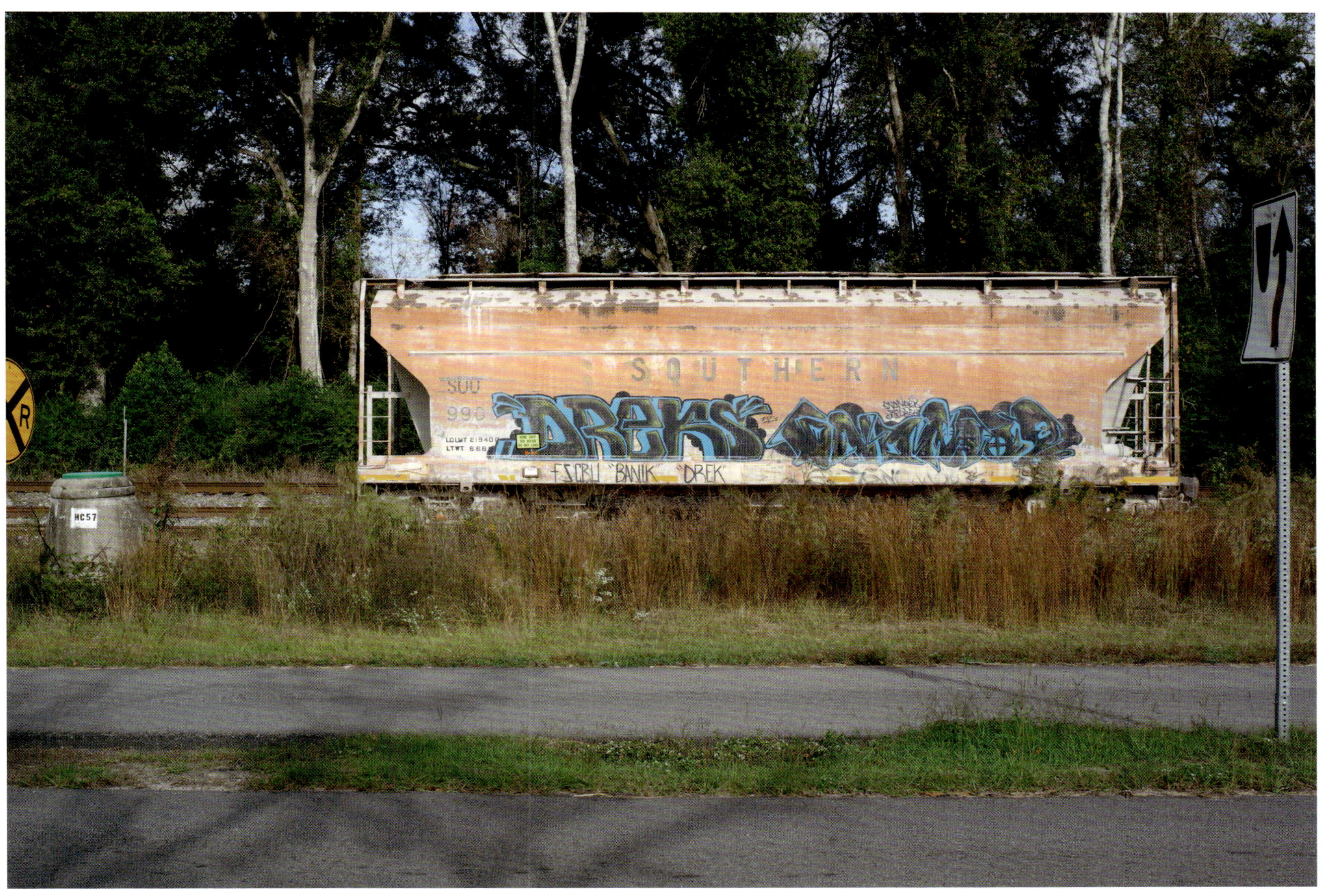

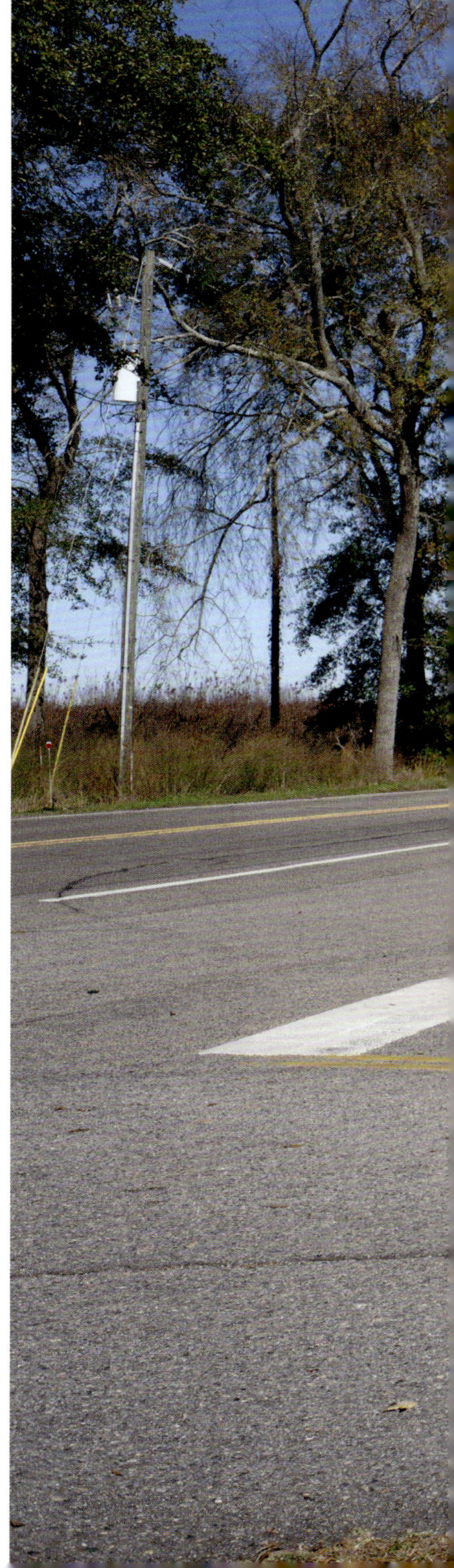

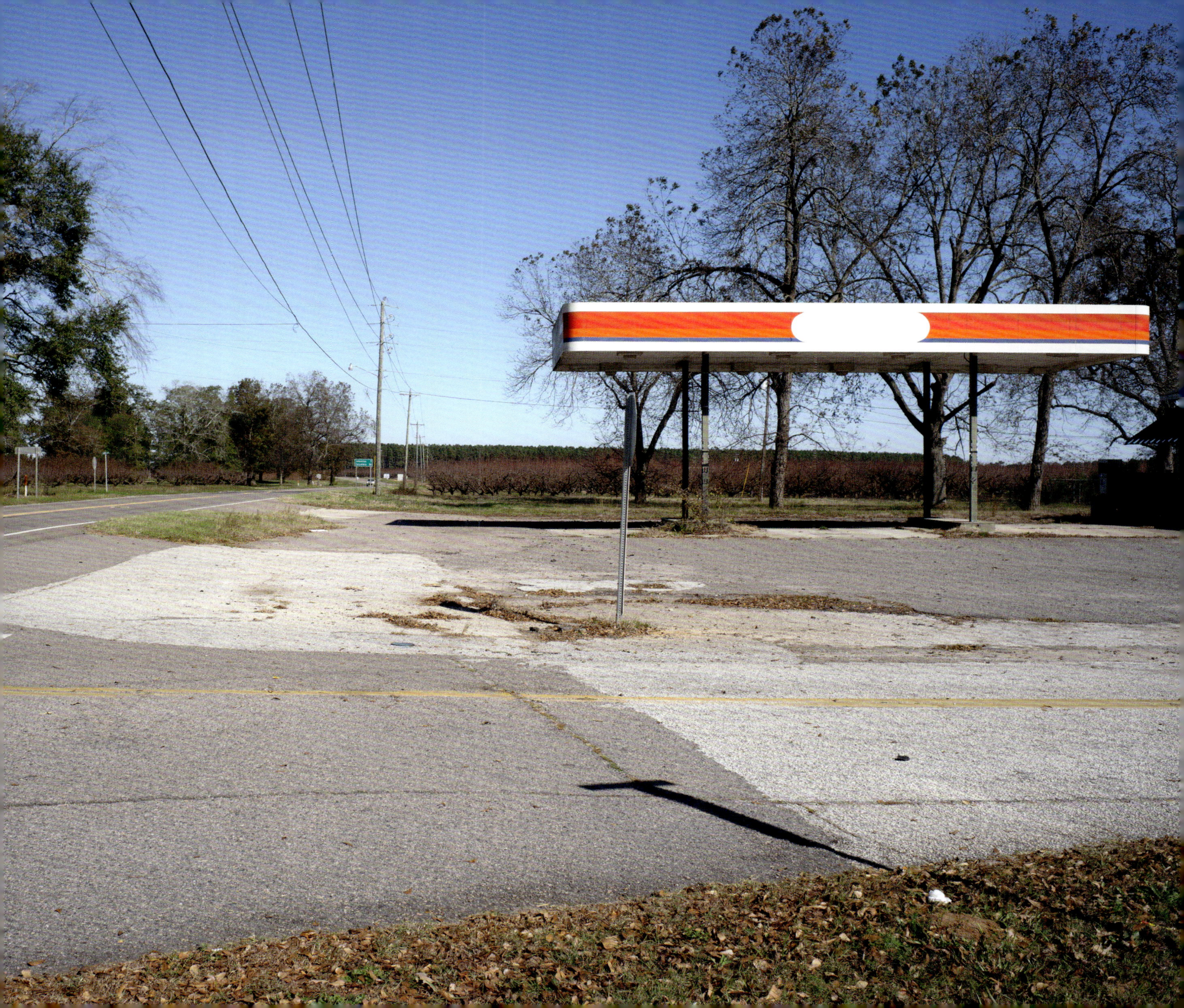

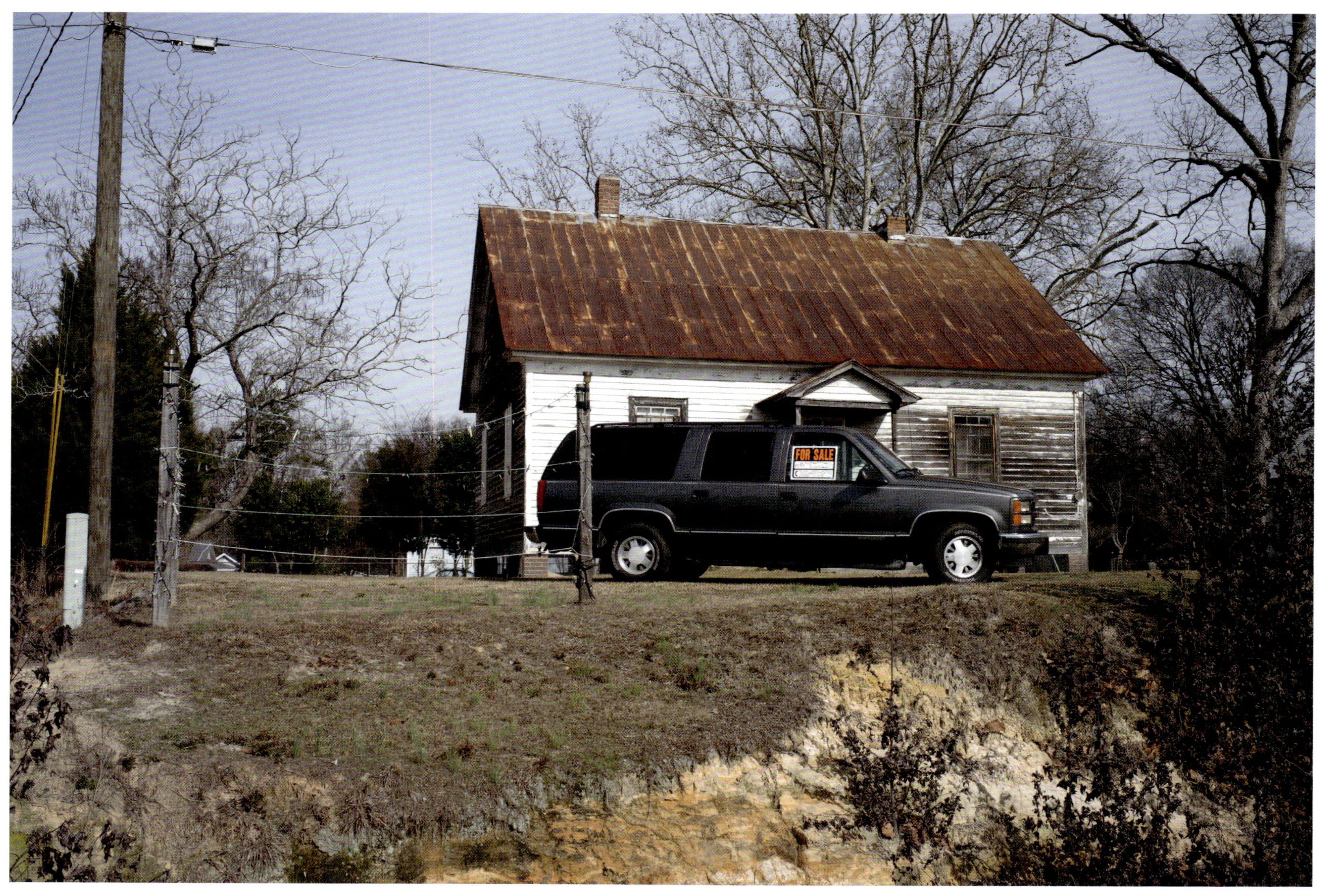

FOR SALE

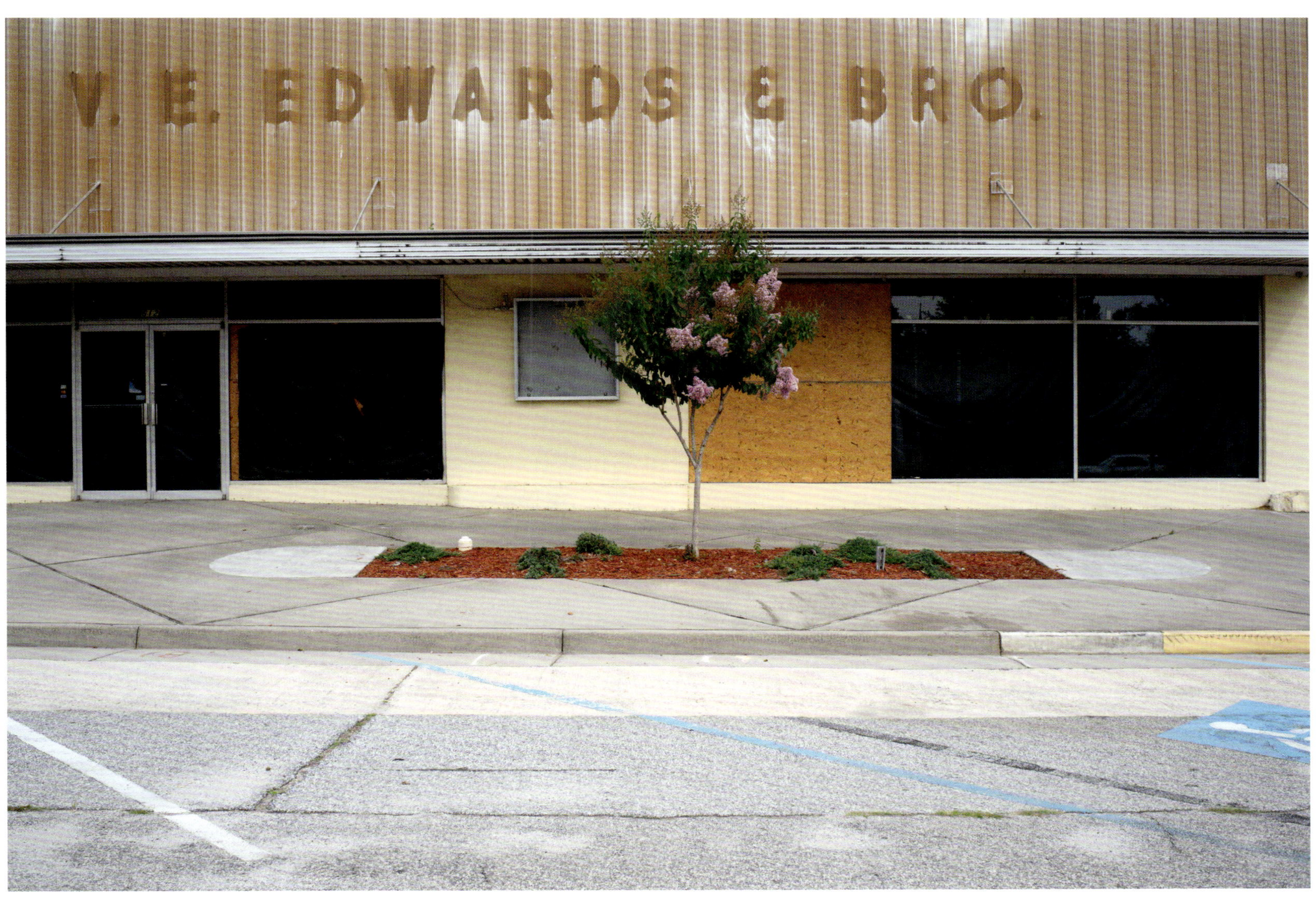
V. E. EDWARDS & BRO.

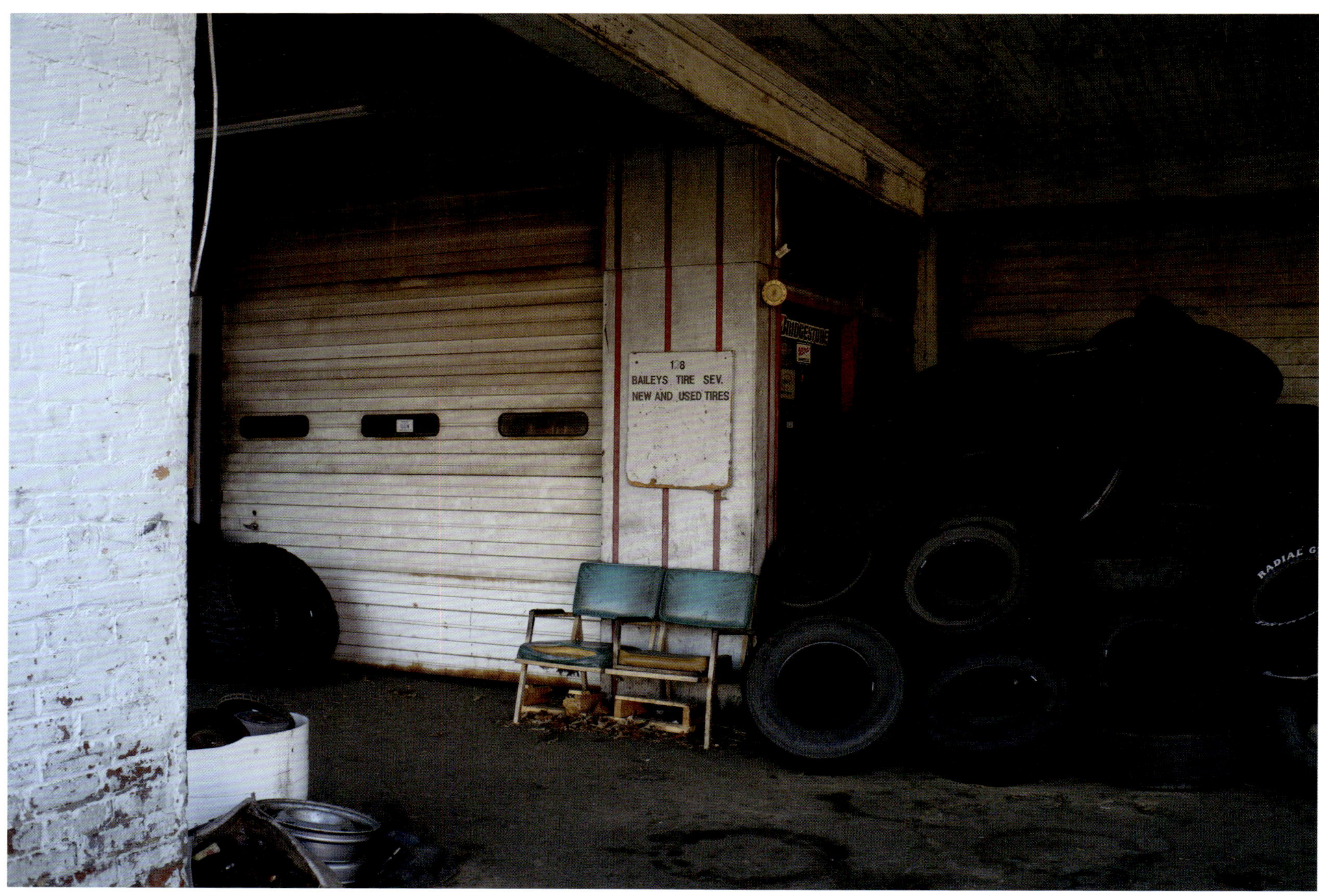
1 8
BAILEYS TIRE SEV.
NEW AND USED TIRES
BRIDGESTONE
RADIAL G

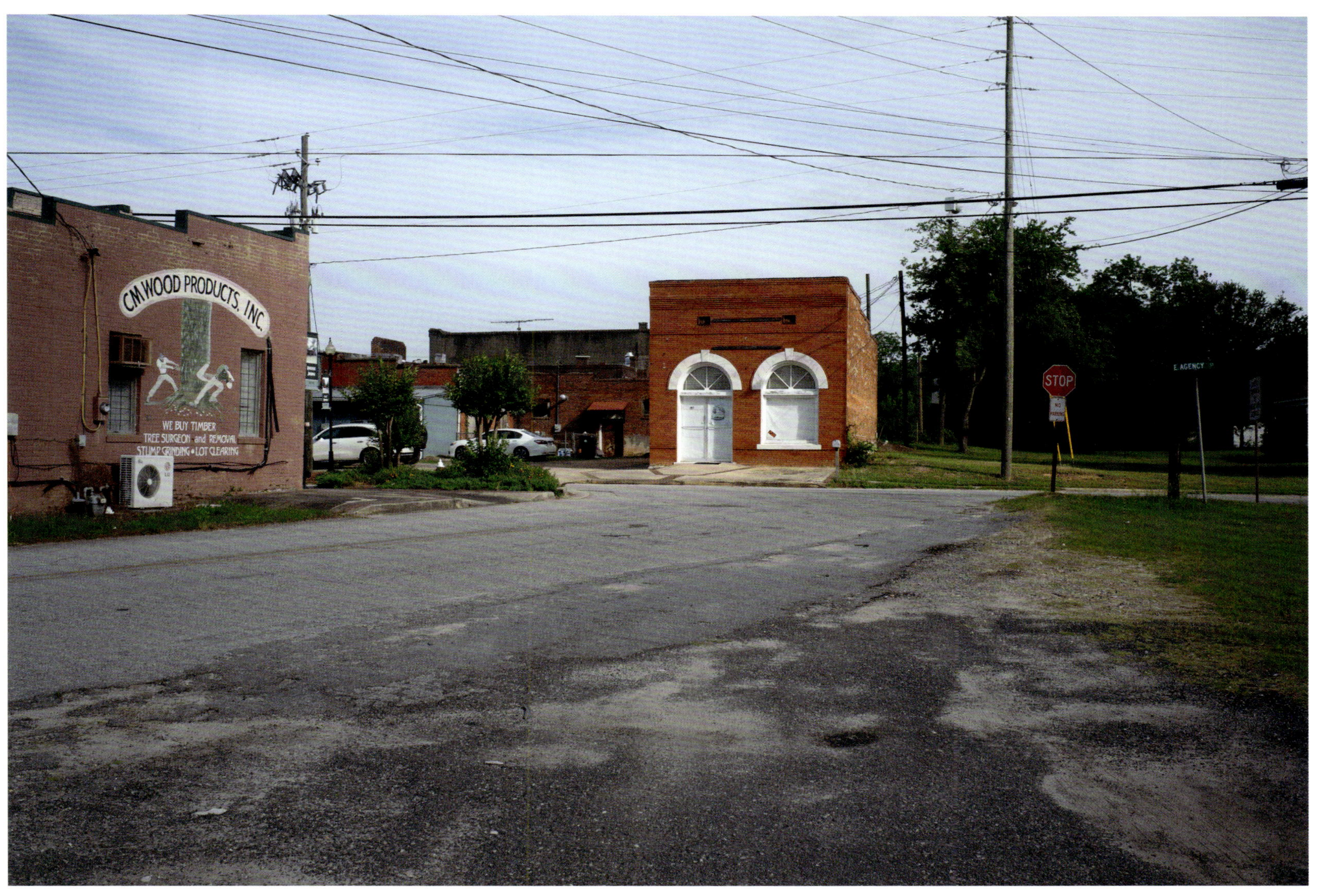
CM WOOD PRODUCTS, INC.
WE BUY TIMBER
TREE SURGEON and REMOVAL
STUMP GRINDING • LOT CLEARING
STOP
E. AGENCY

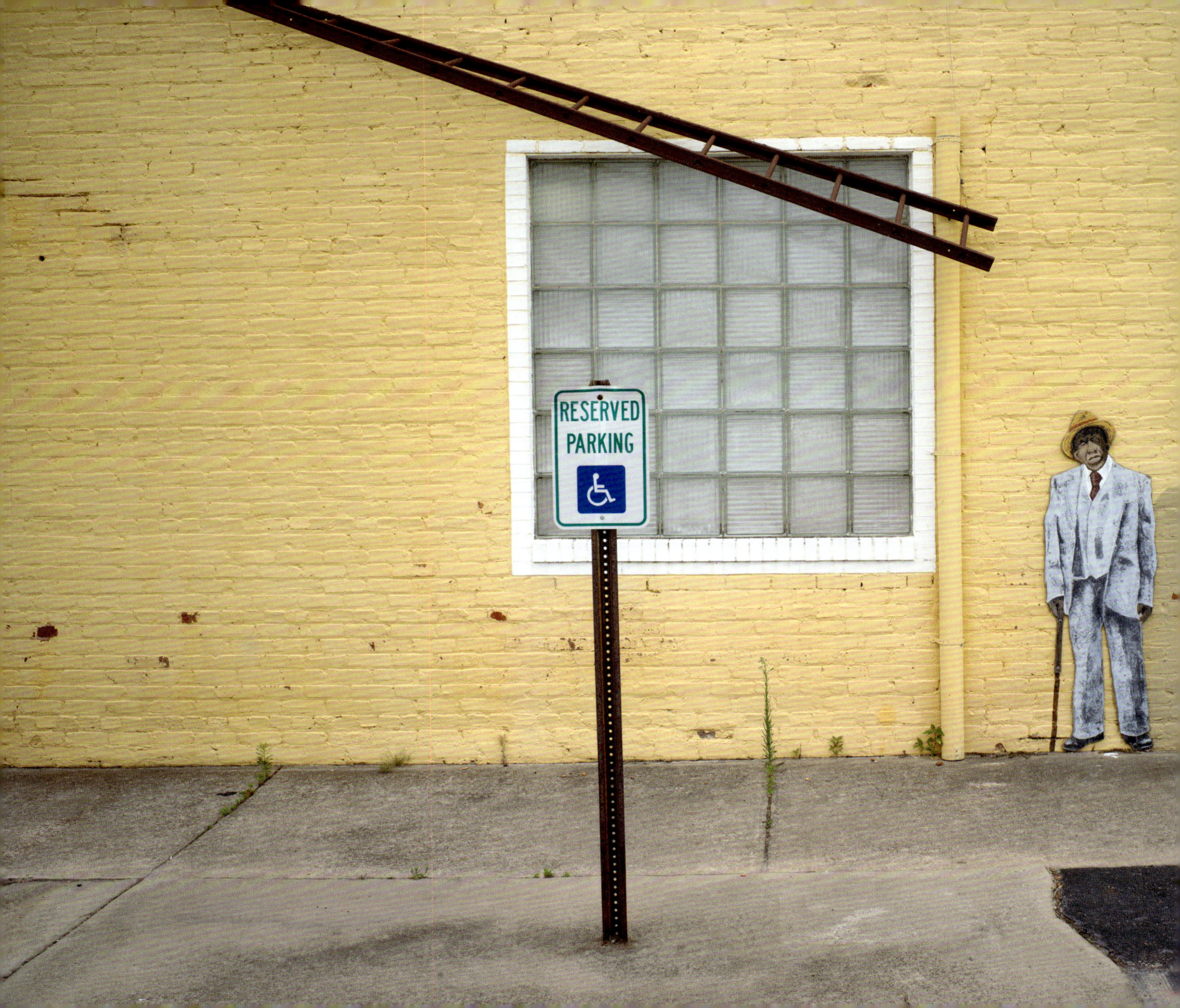
RESERVED
PARKING

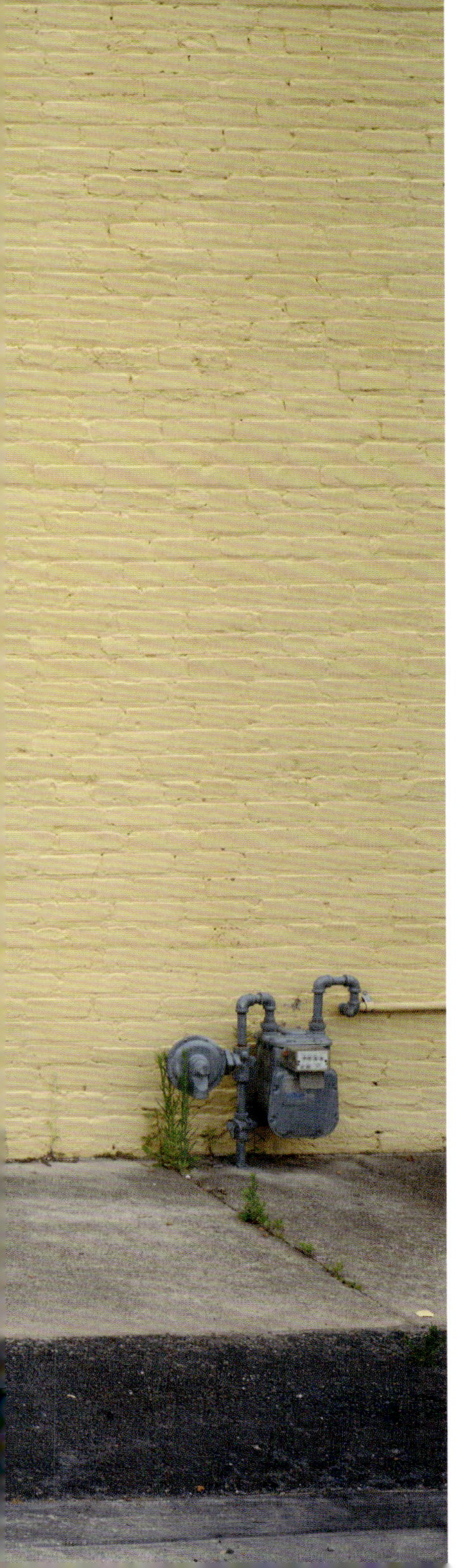

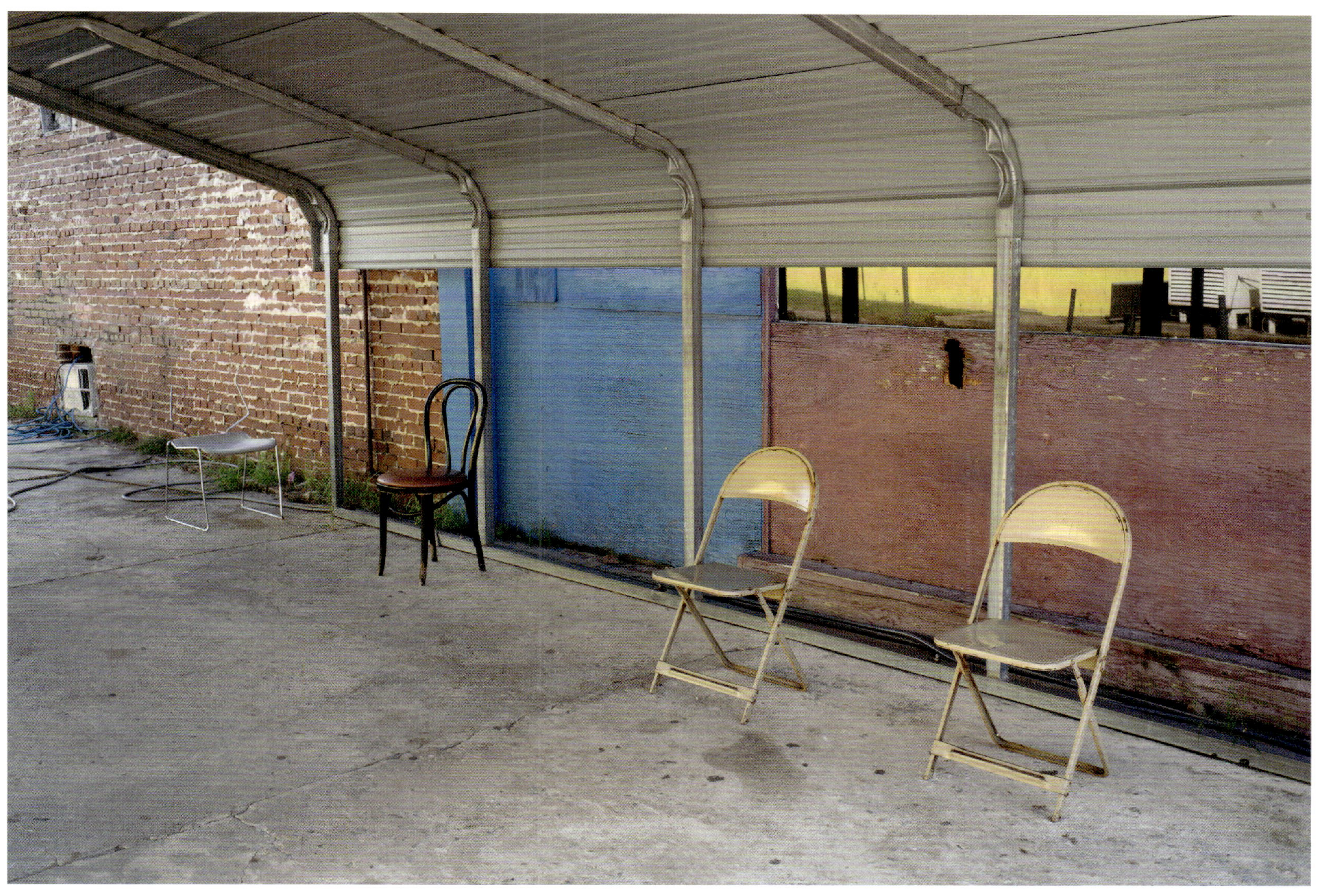

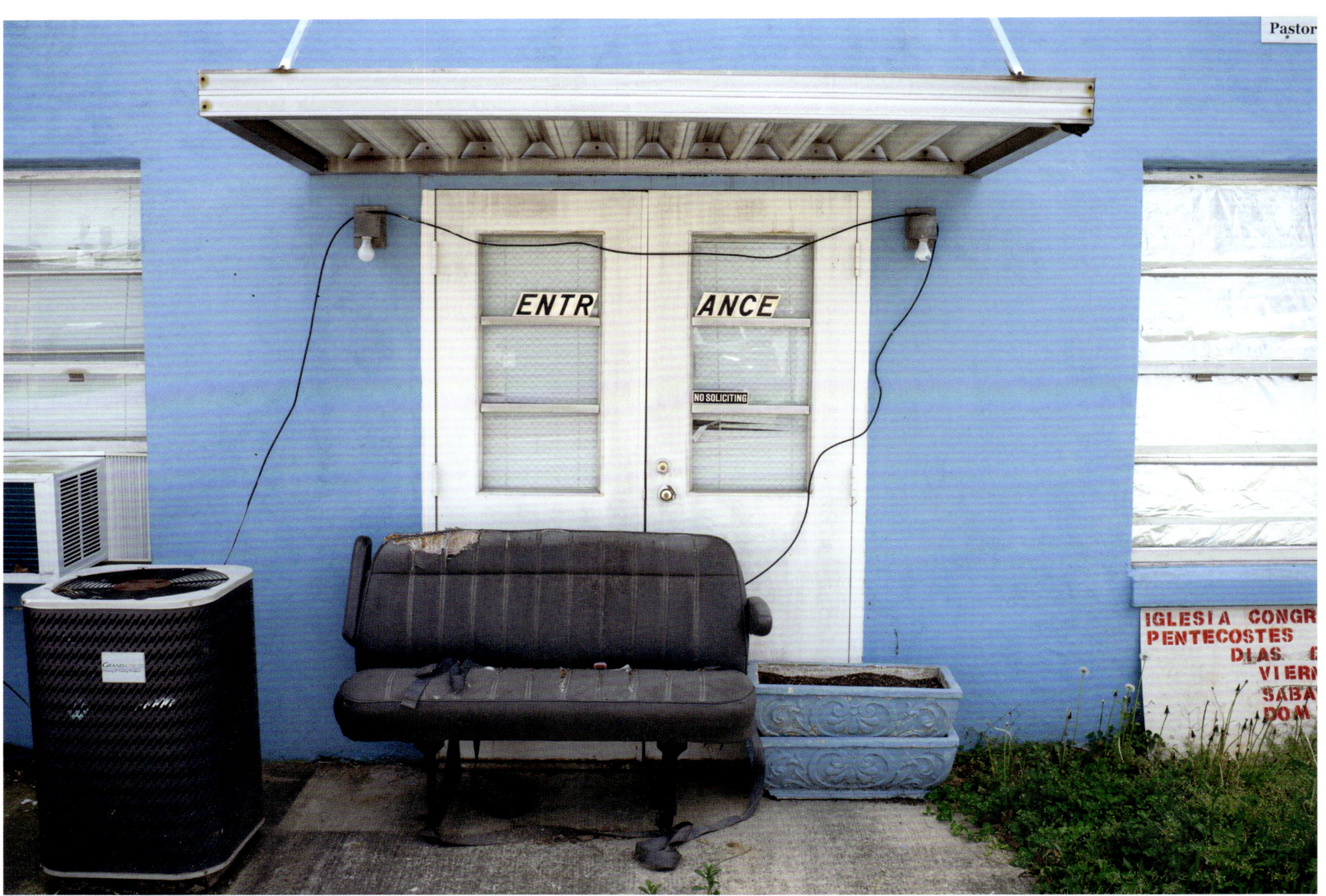

Pastor
ENTR ANCE
NO SOLICITING
IGLESIA CONGR
PENTECOSTES
DIAS
VIERN
SABA
DOM

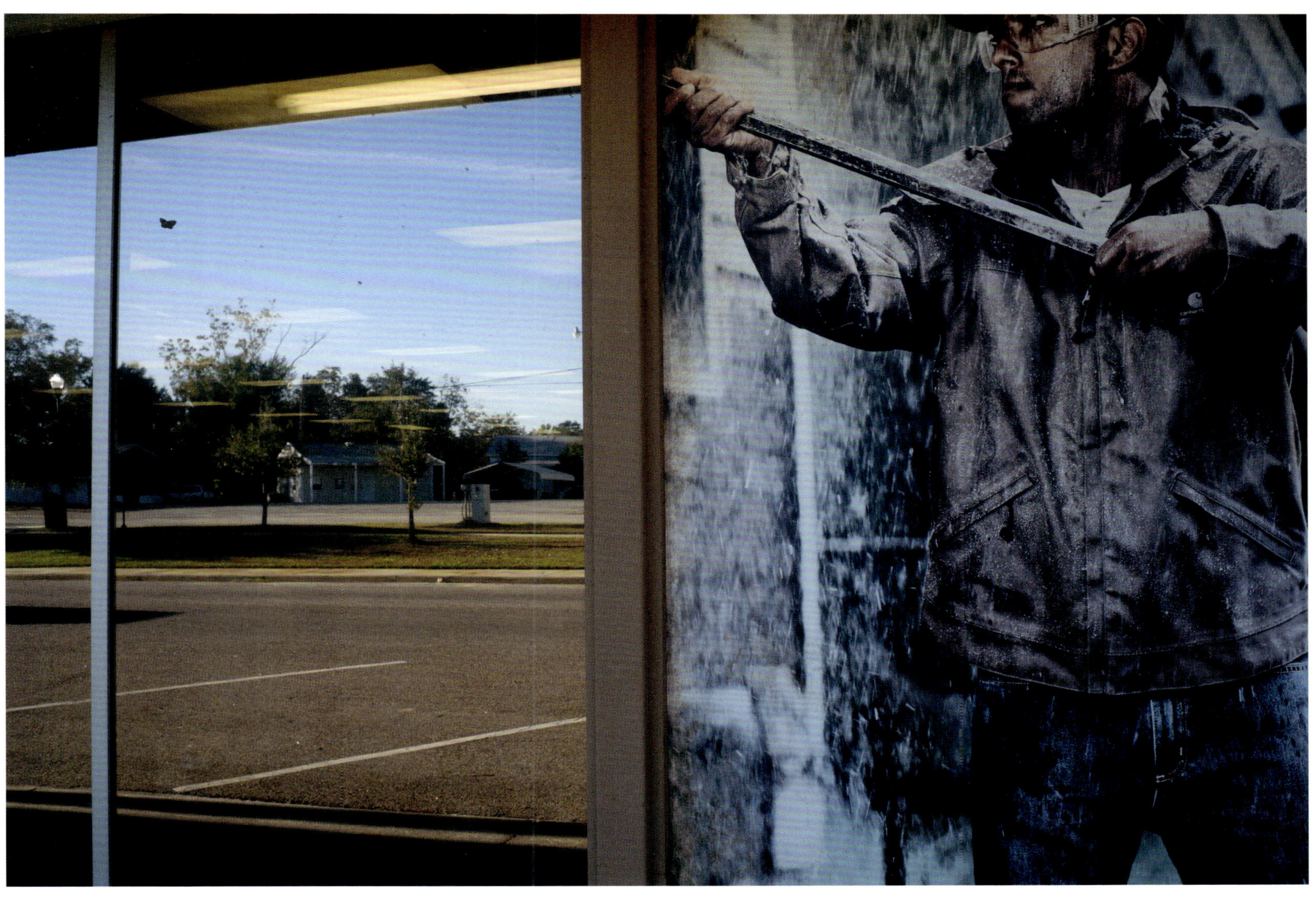

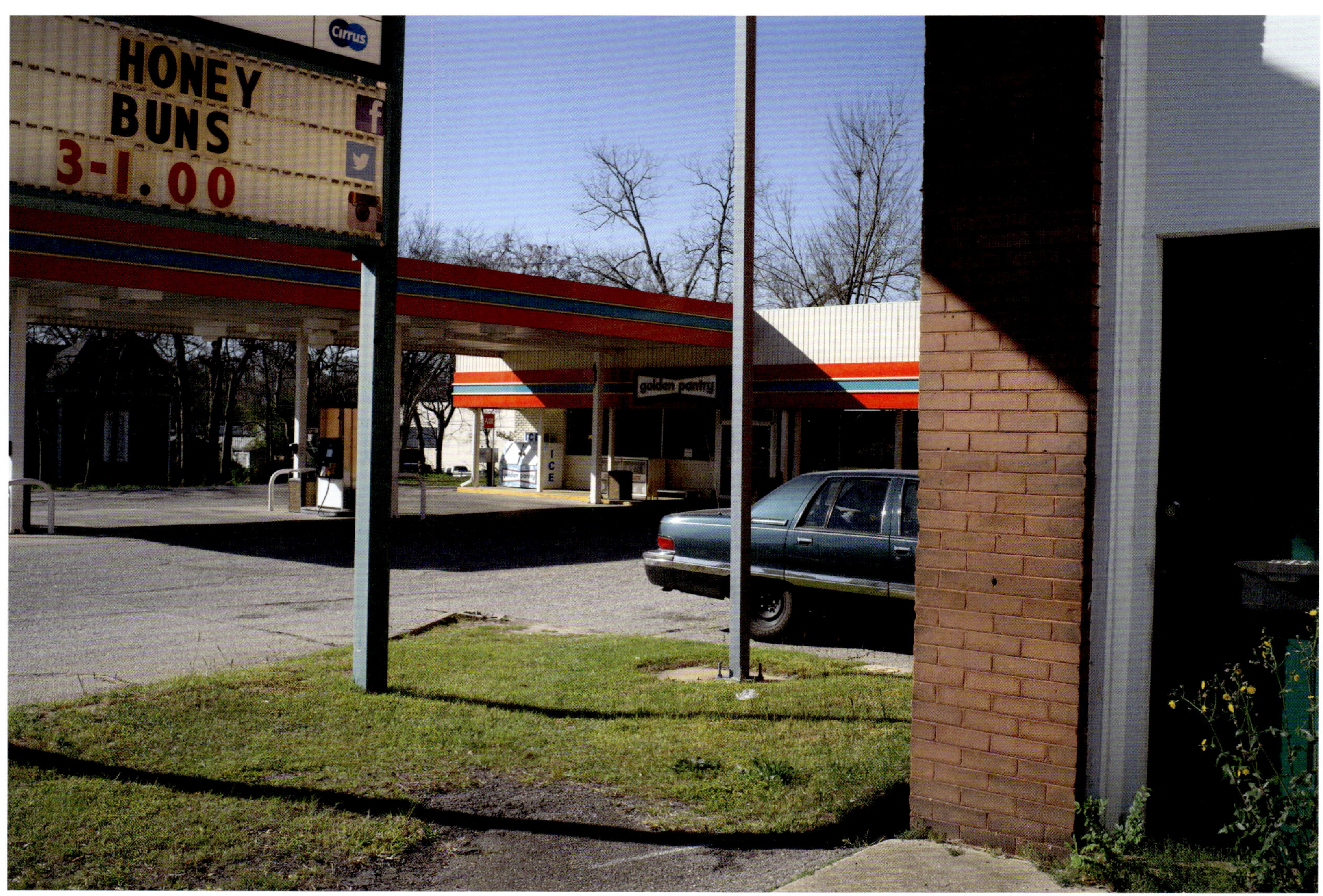

HONEY
BUNS
3-1.00
Cirrus
golden pantry
ICE

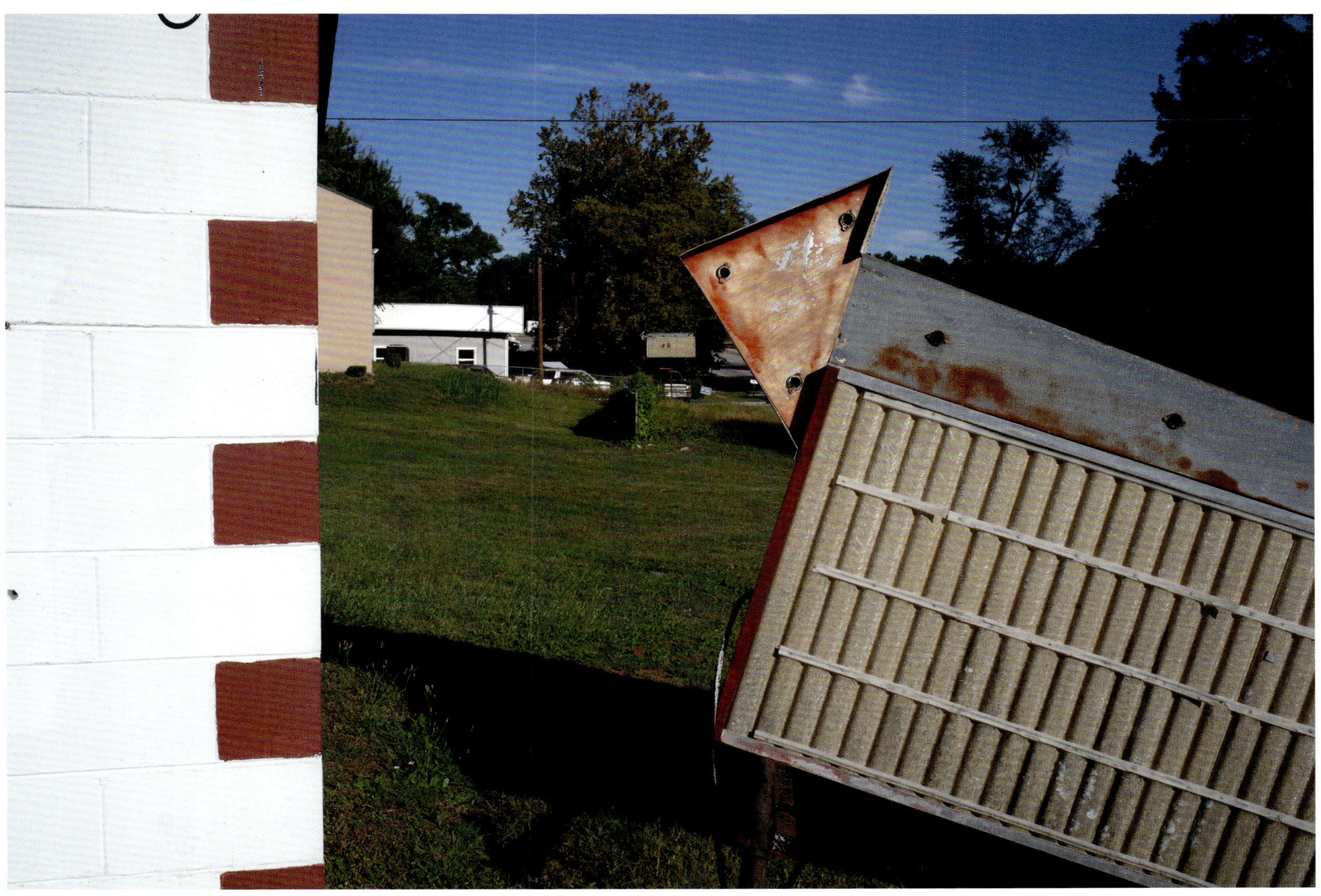

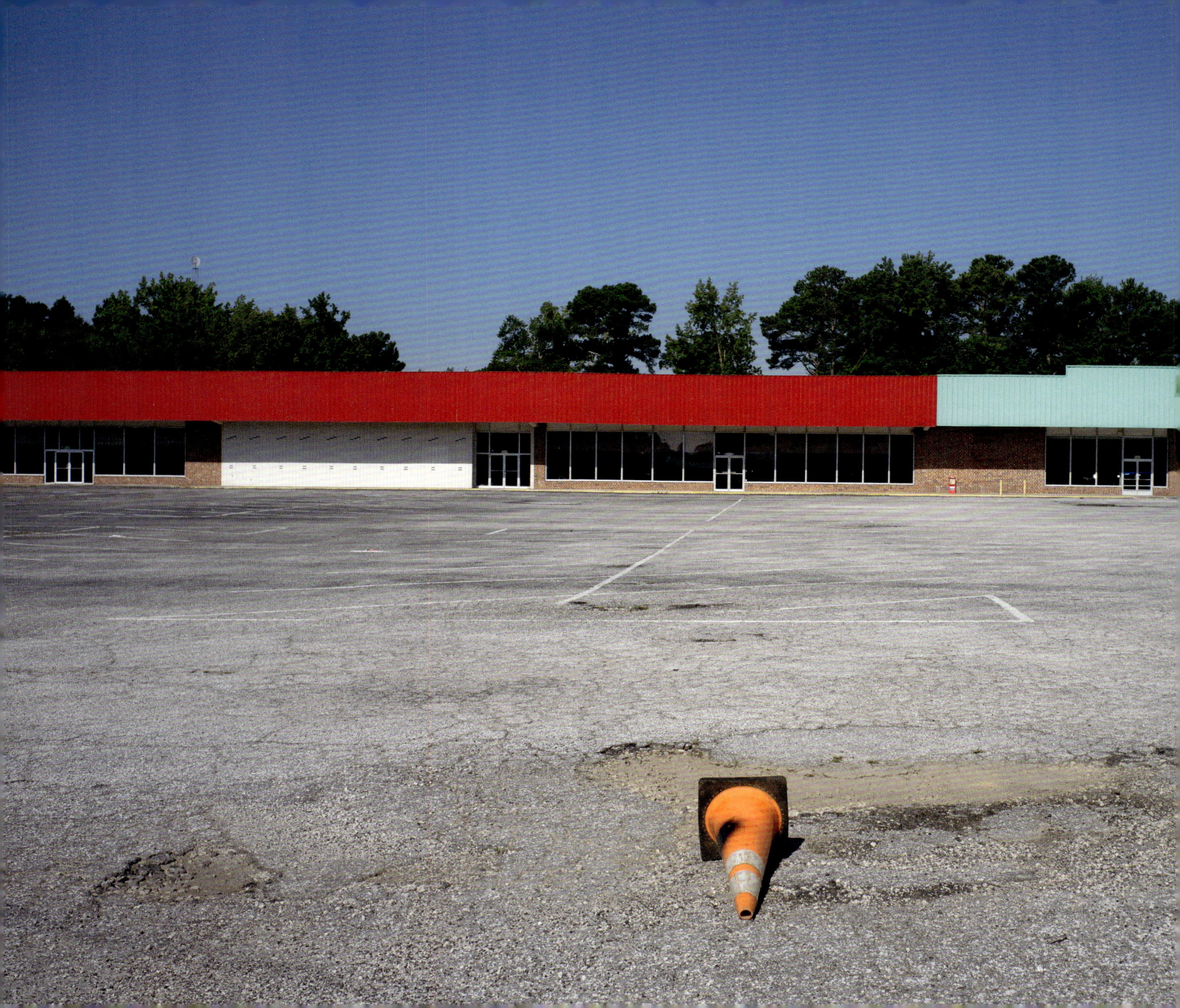

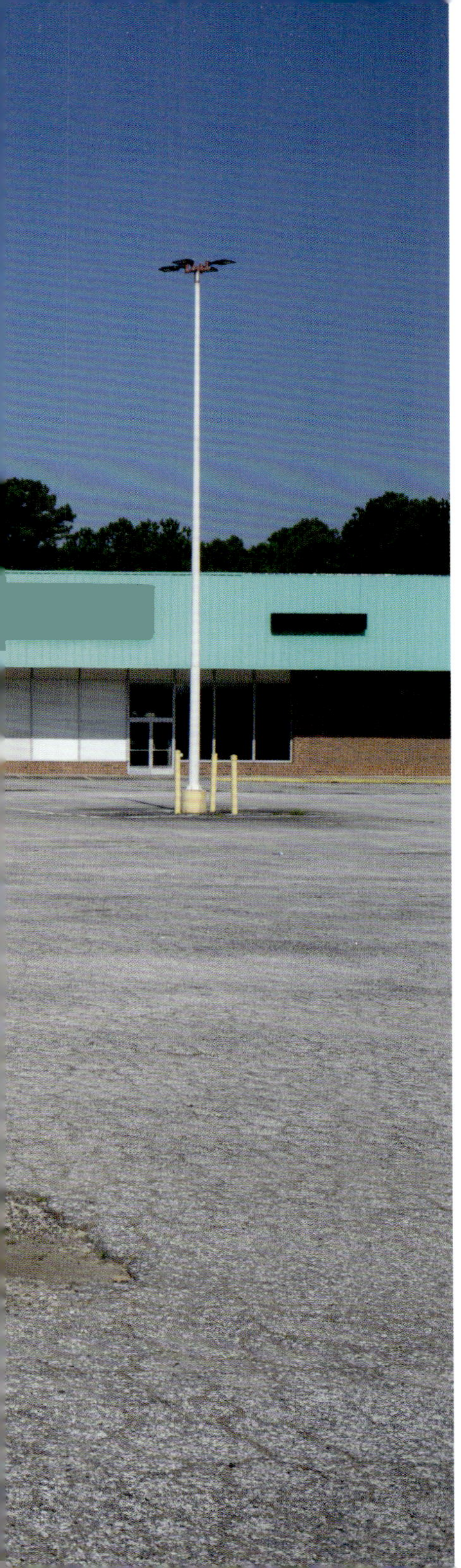

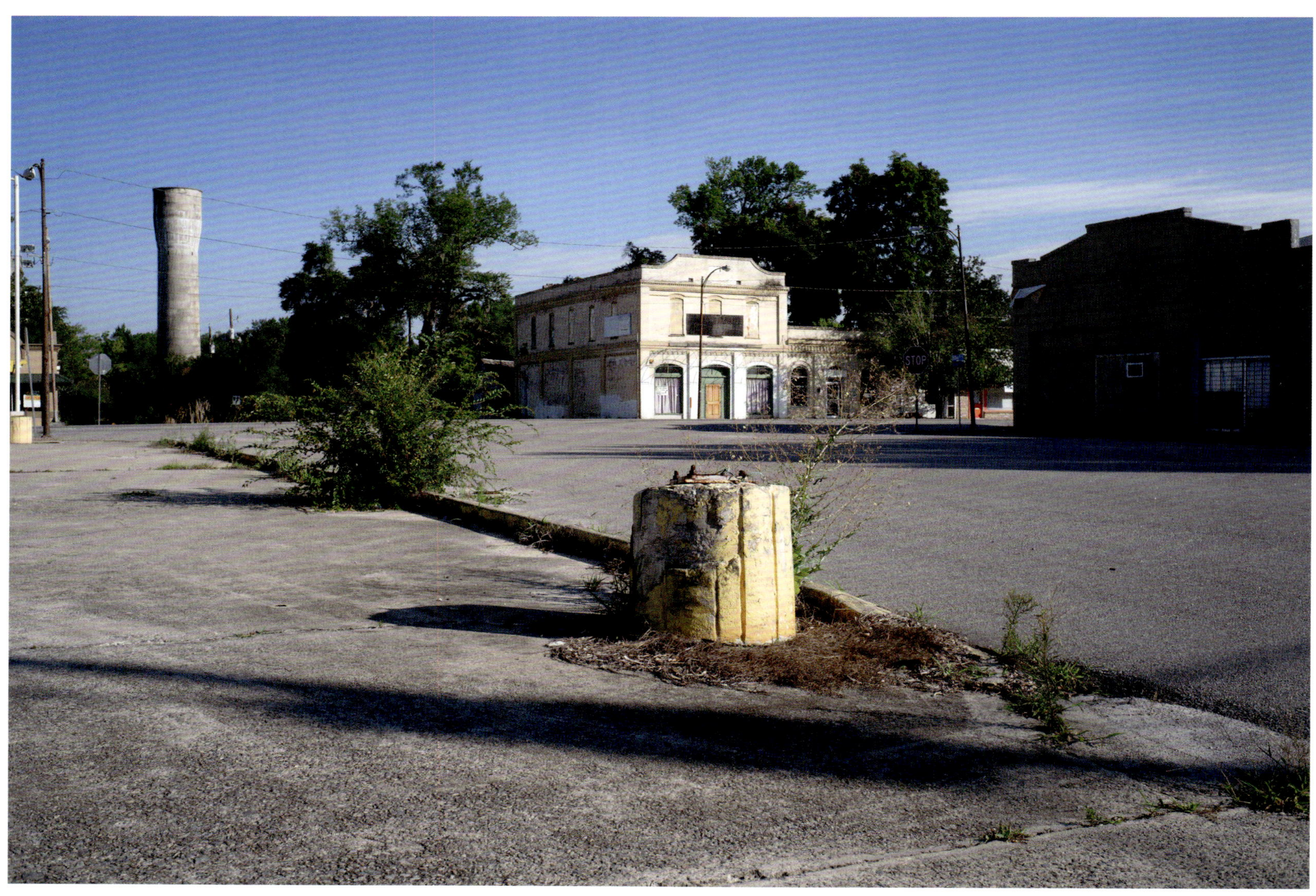

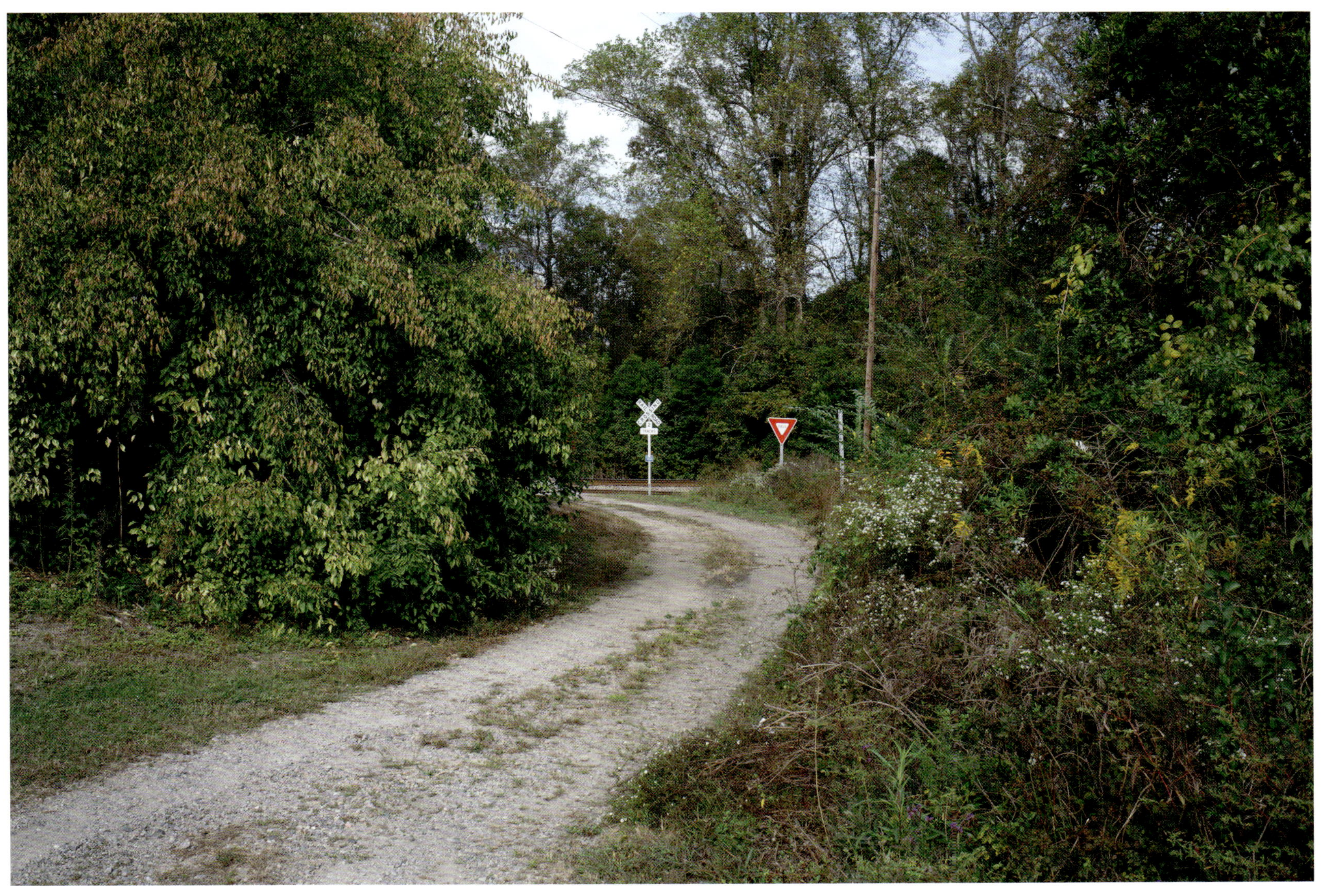

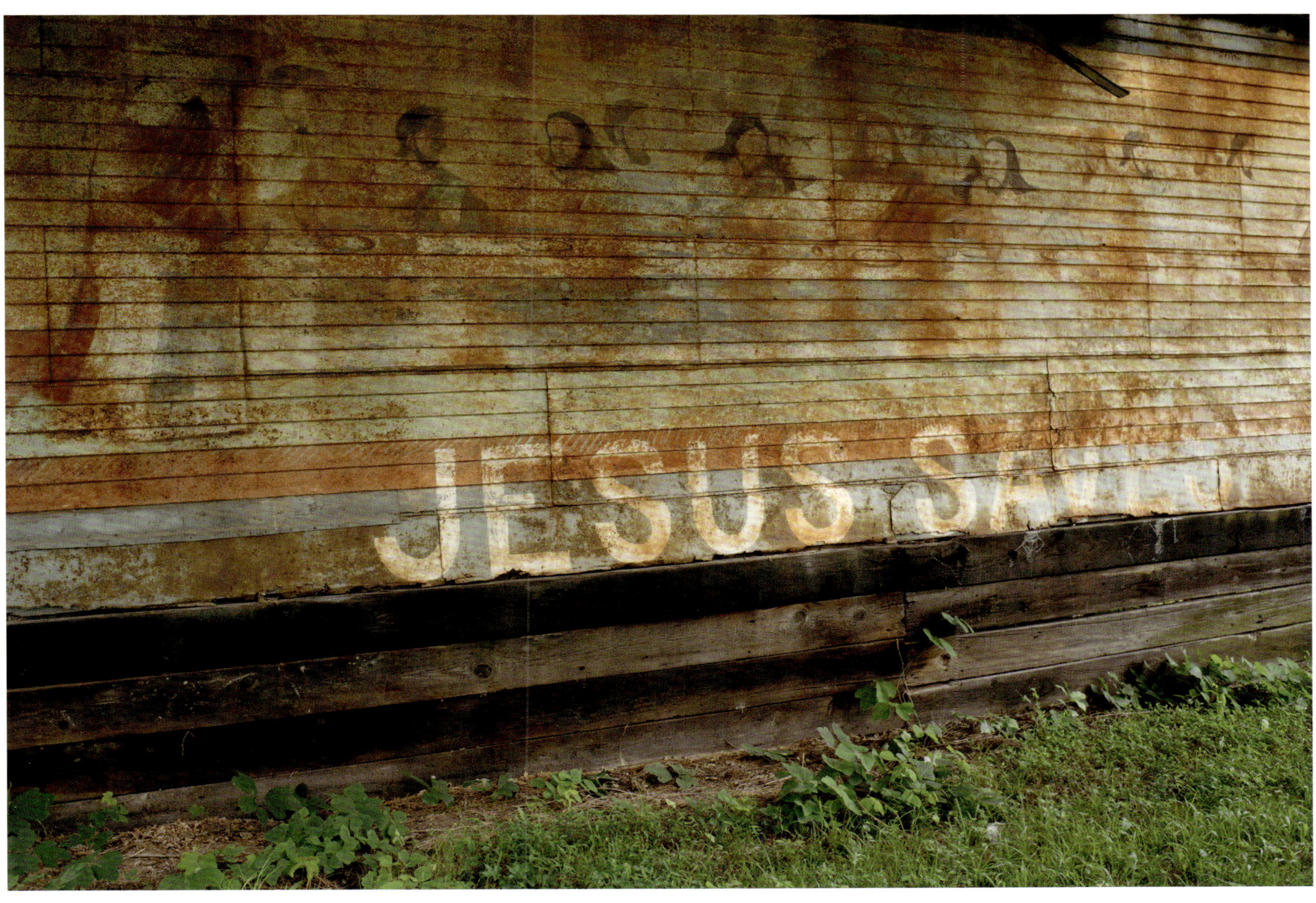

JESUS SAVES

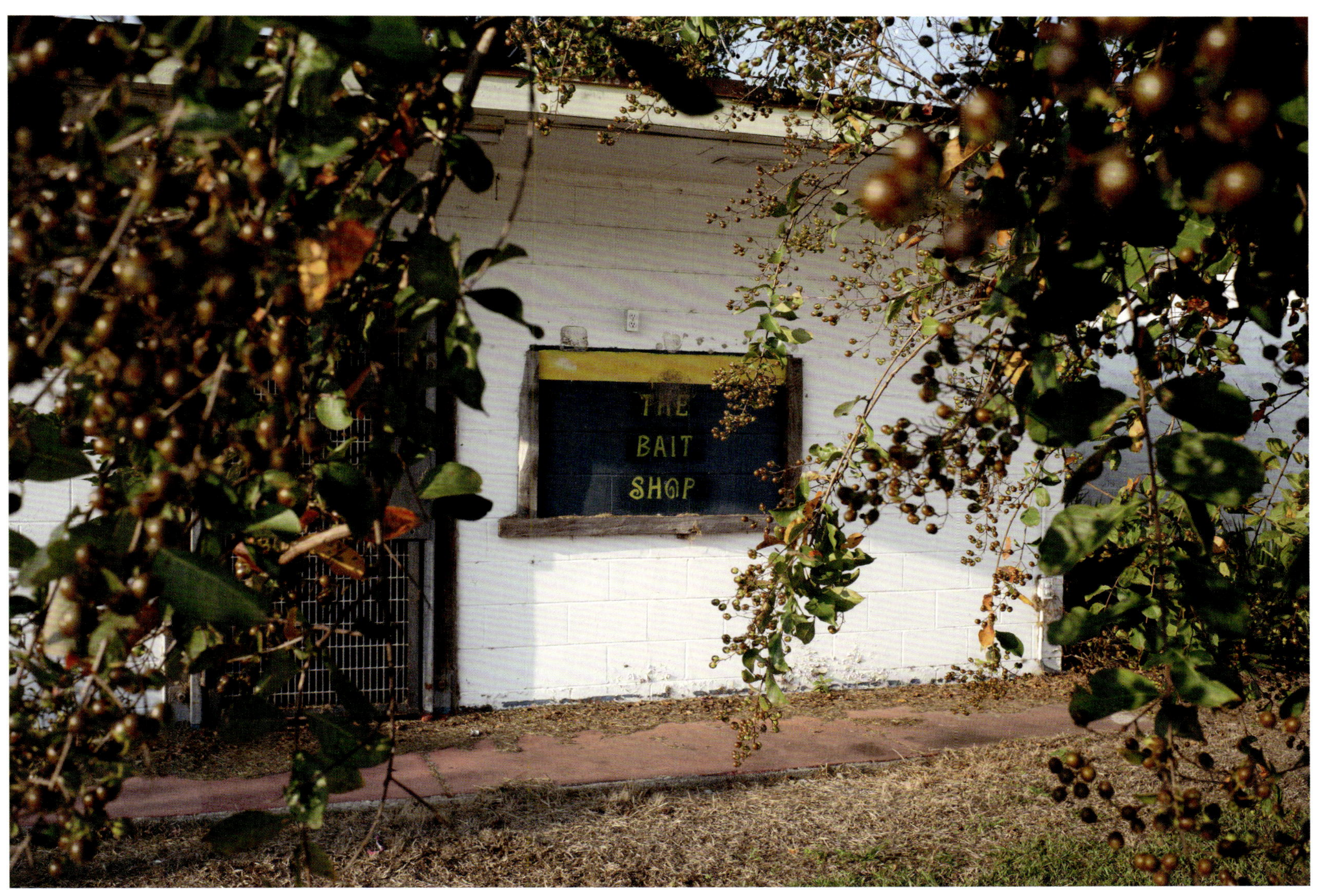
THE
BAIT
SHOP

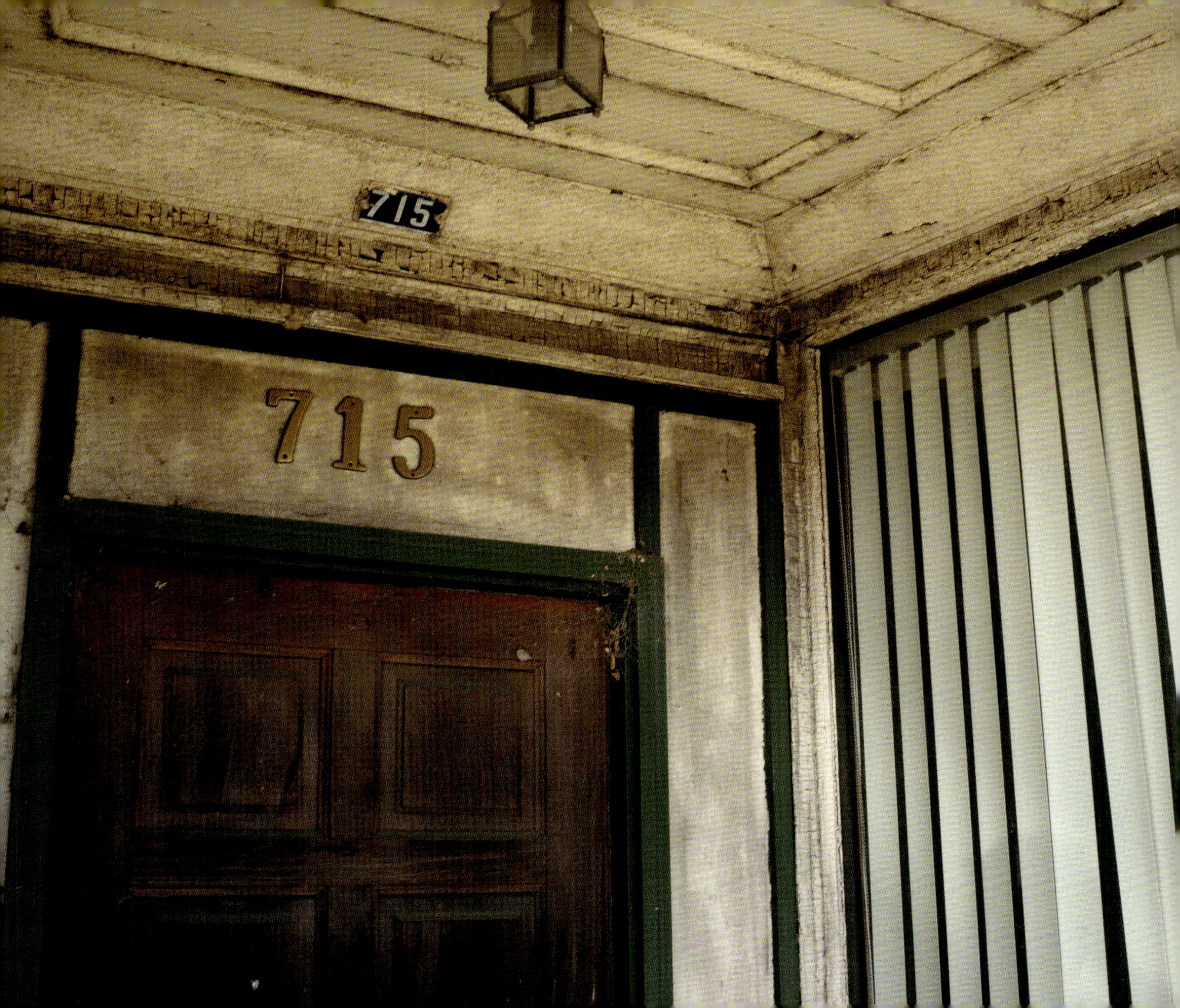
715
715

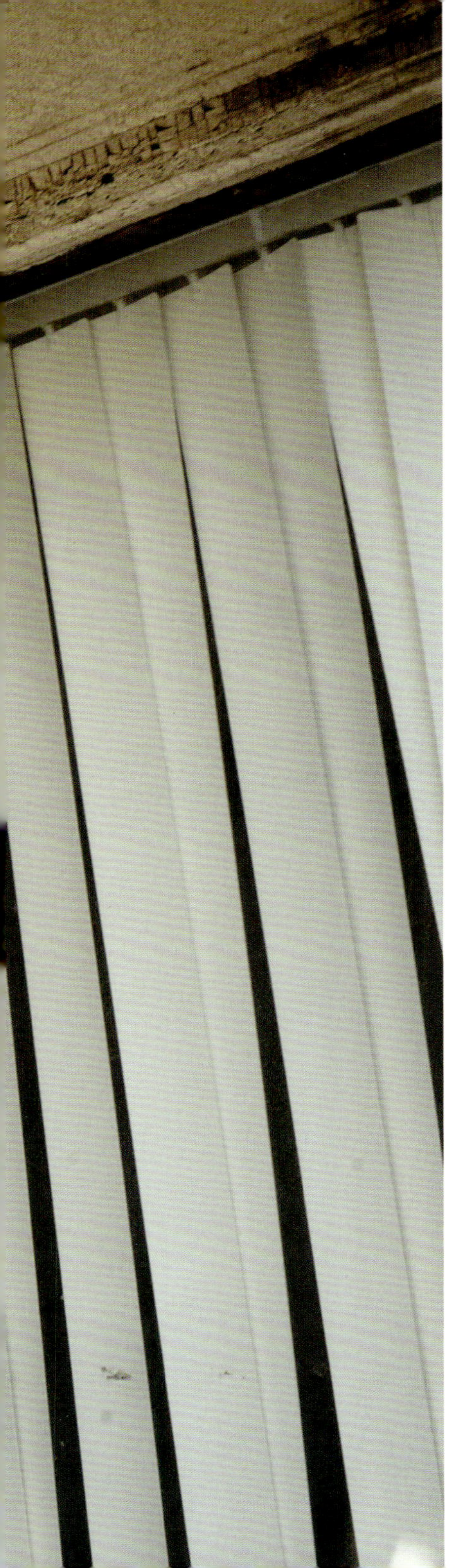

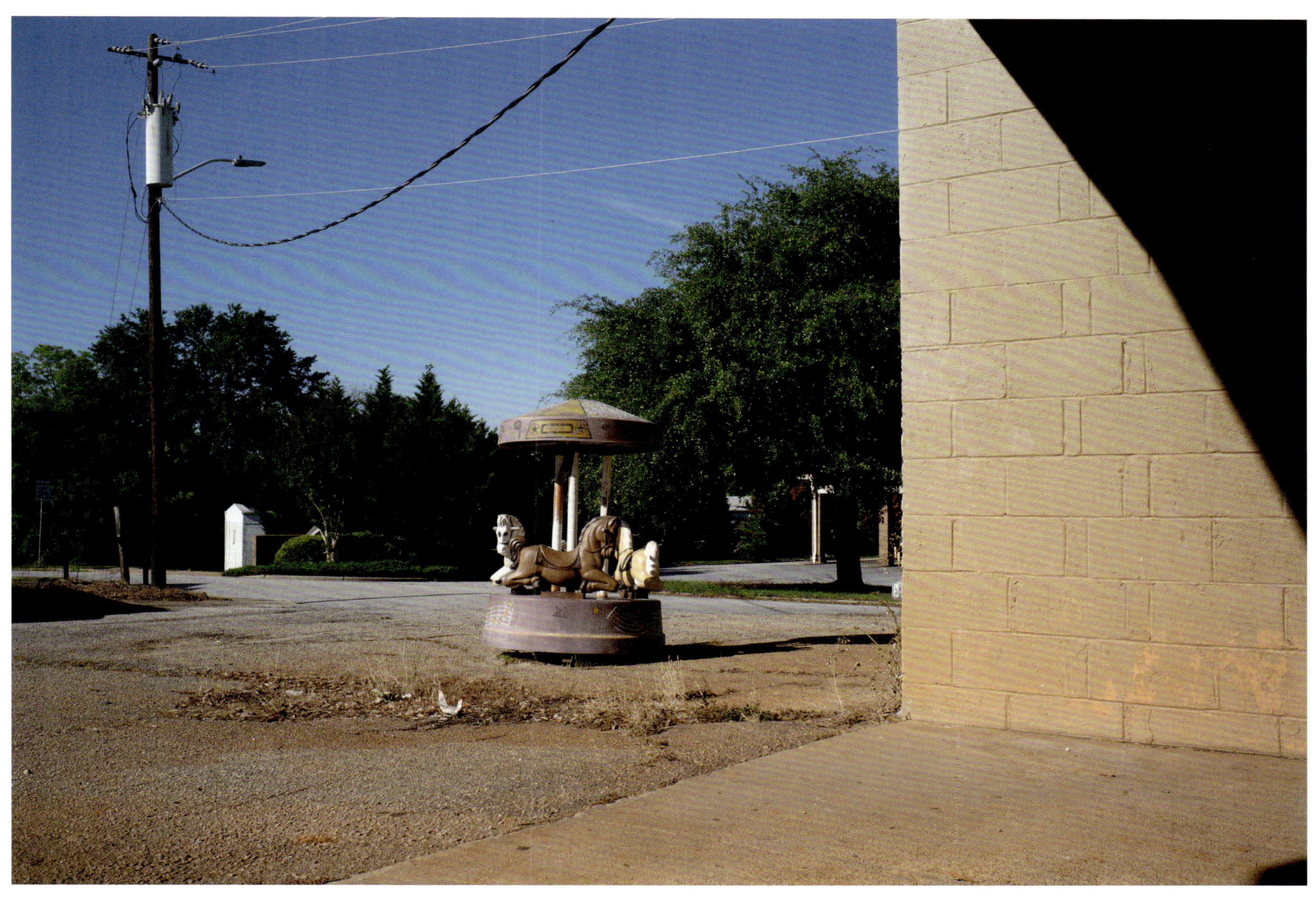

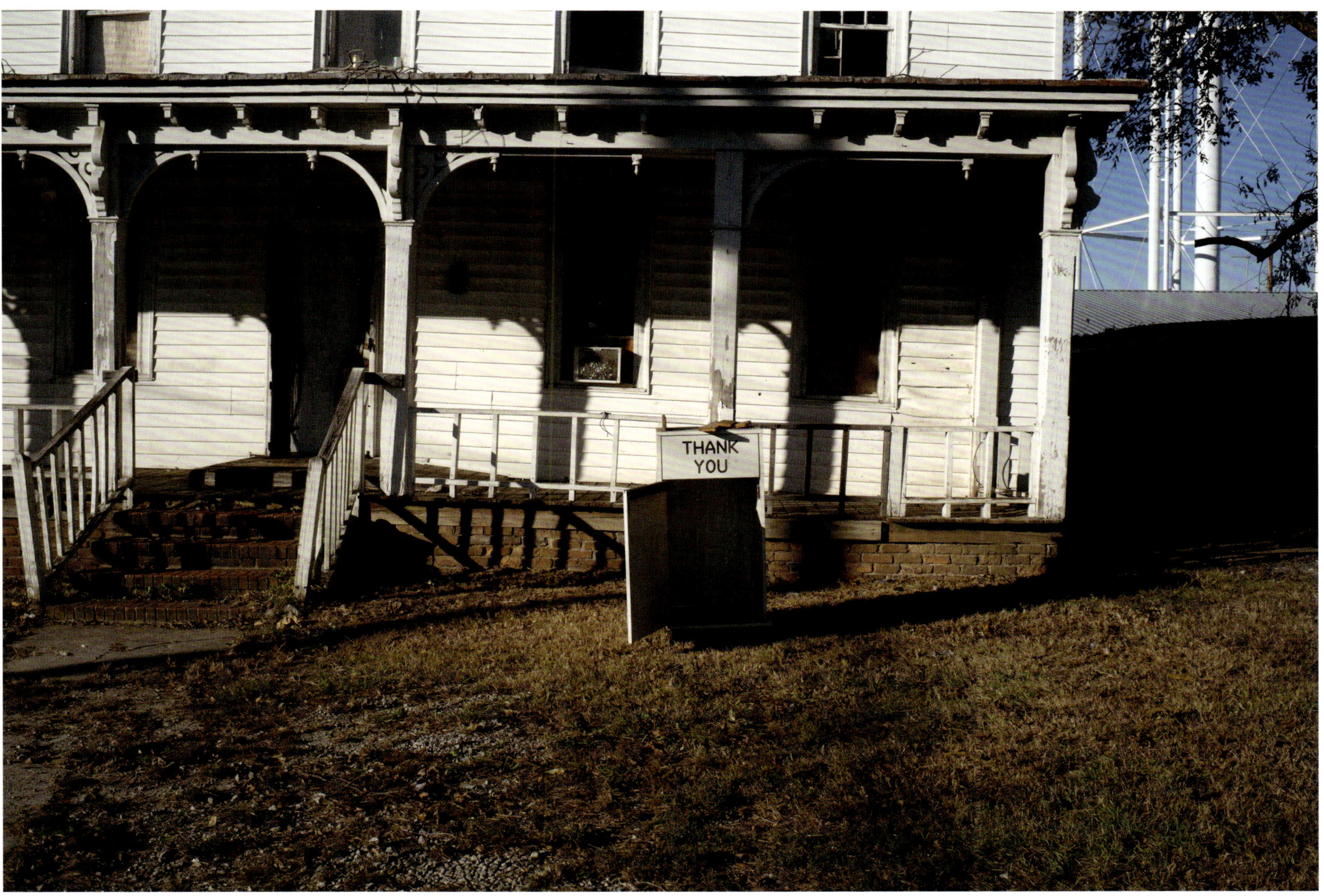
THANK
YOU

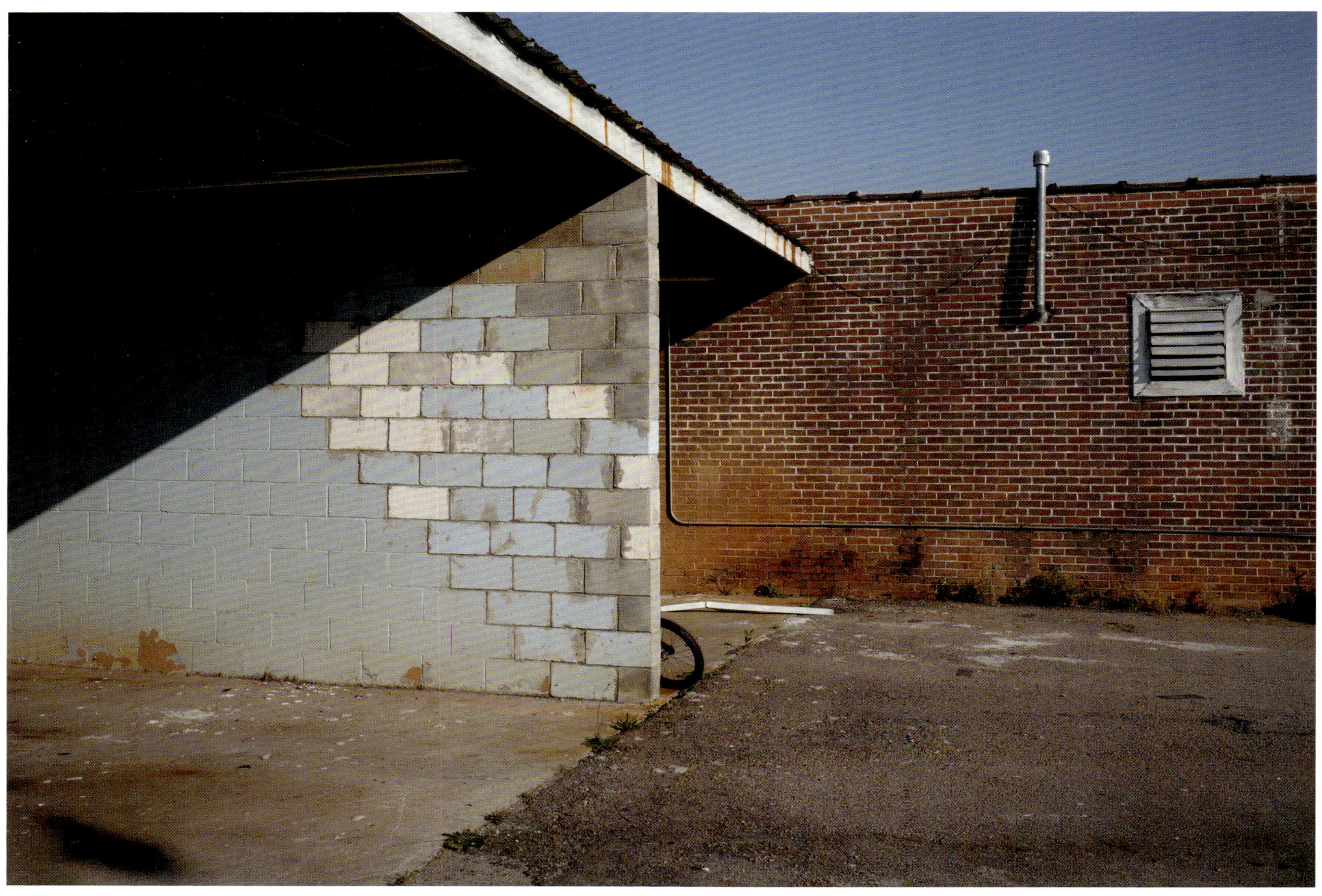

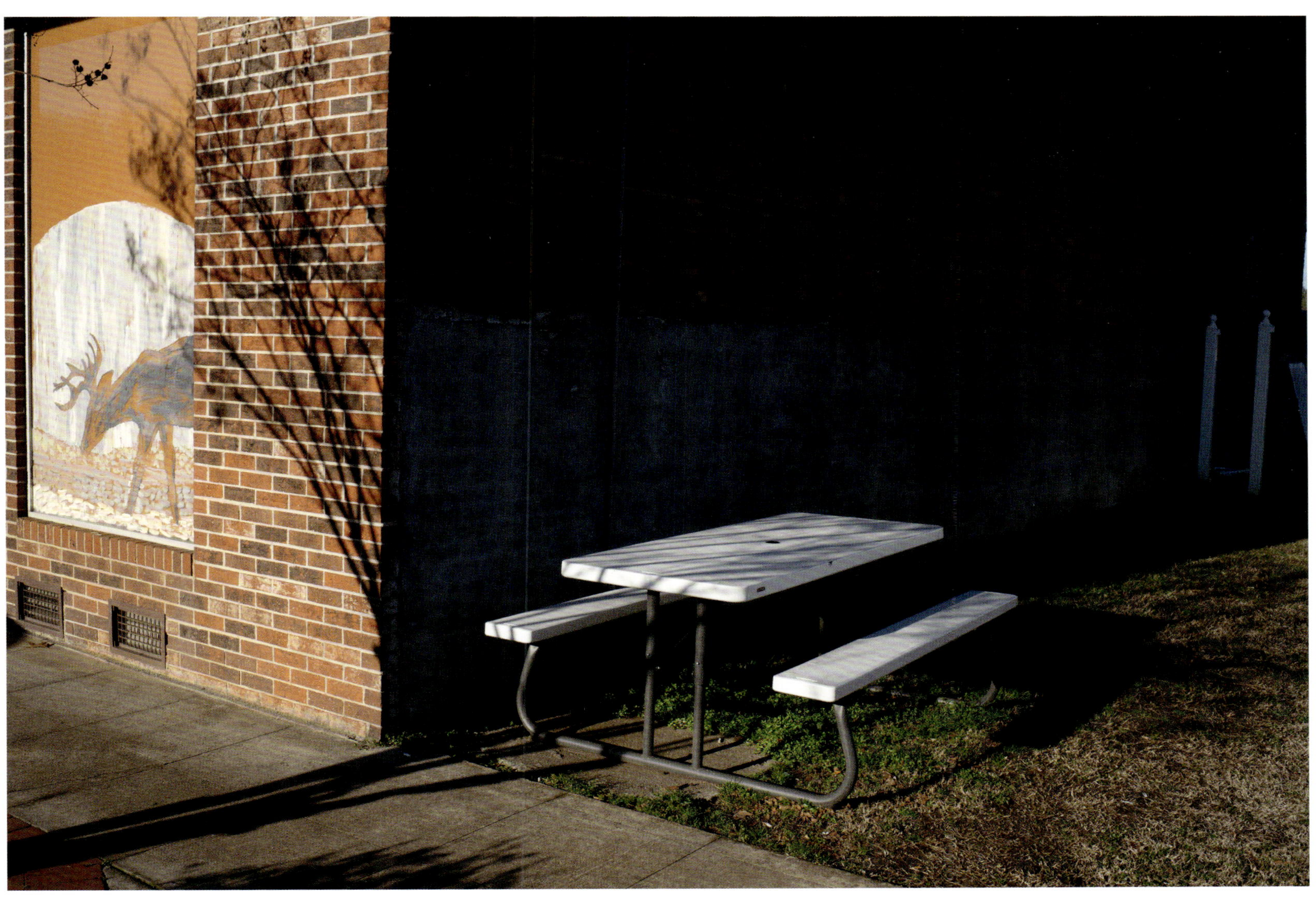

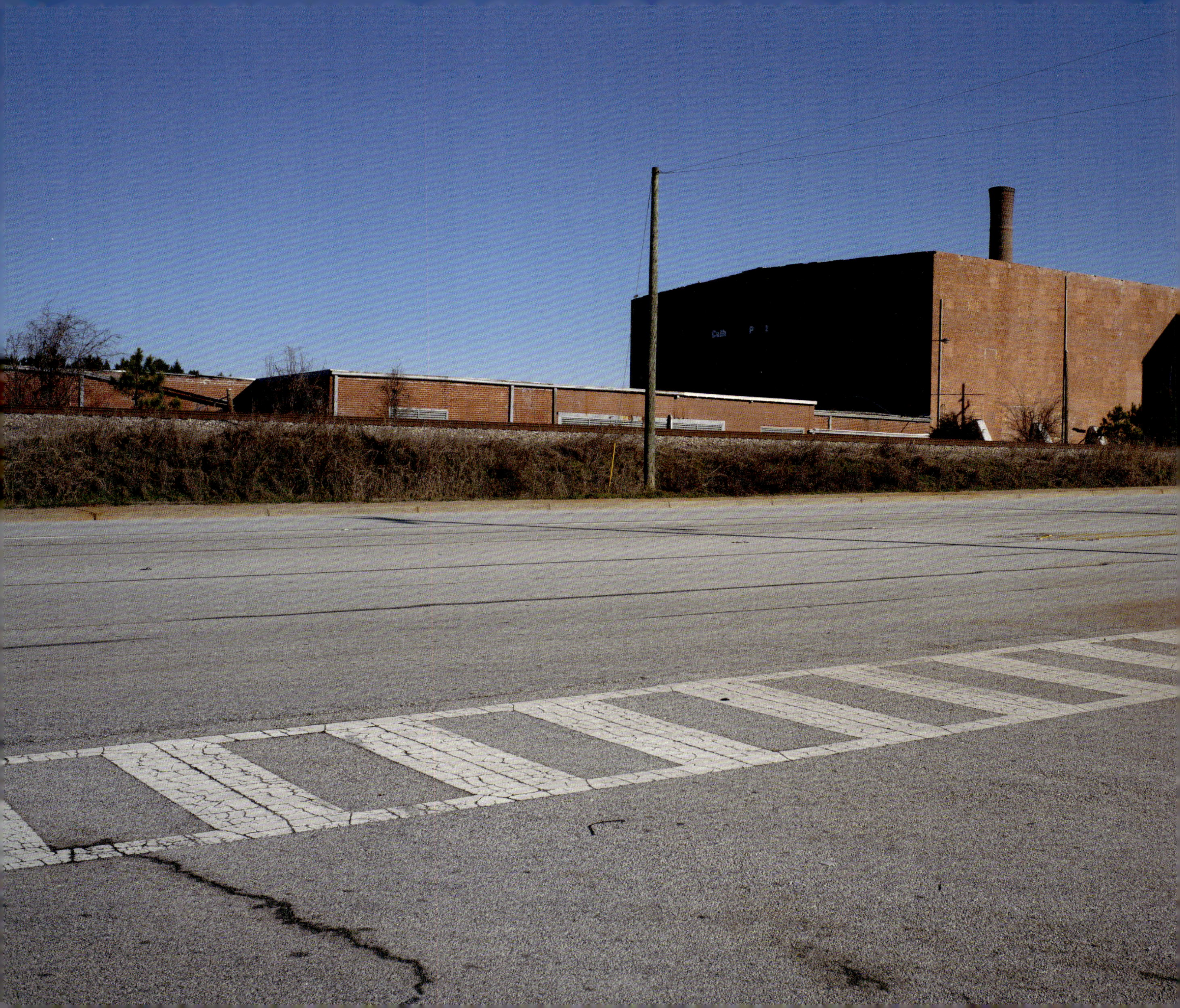

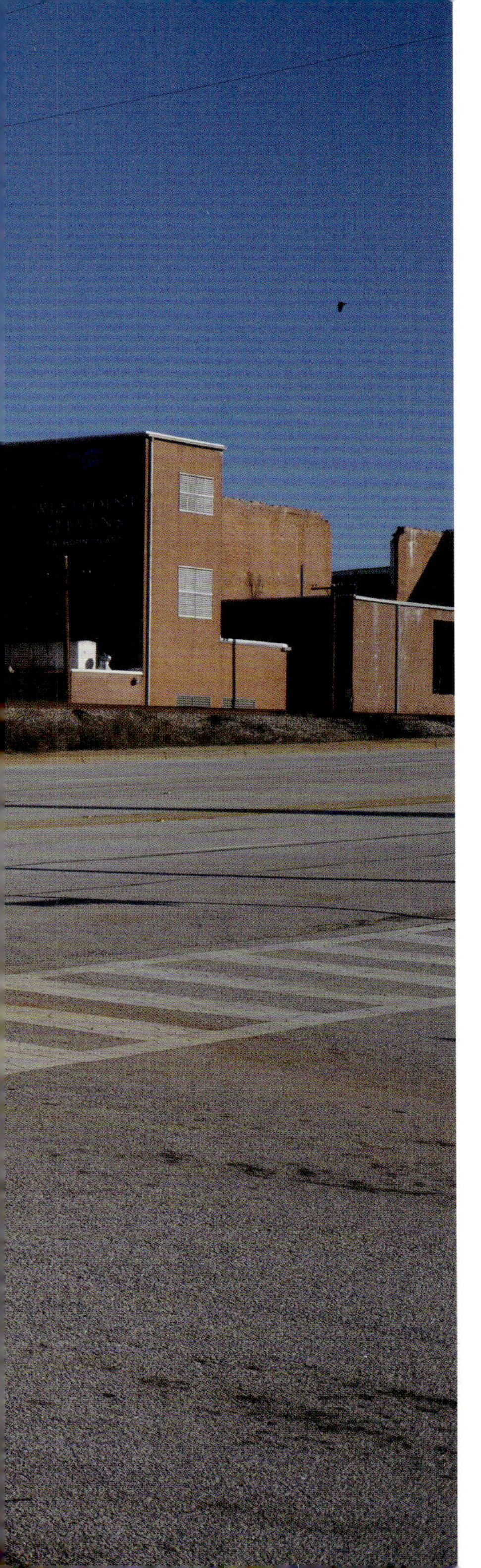

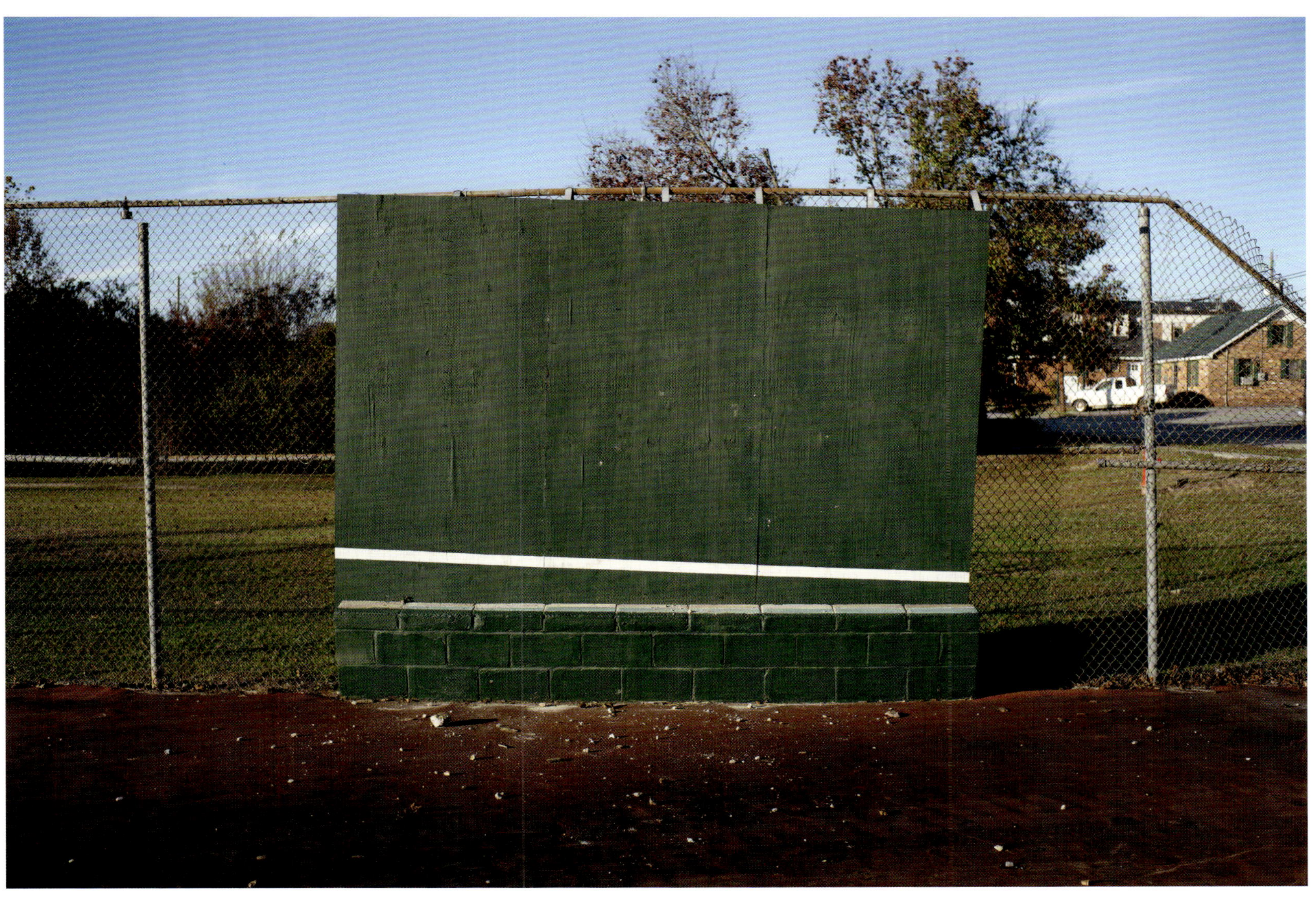

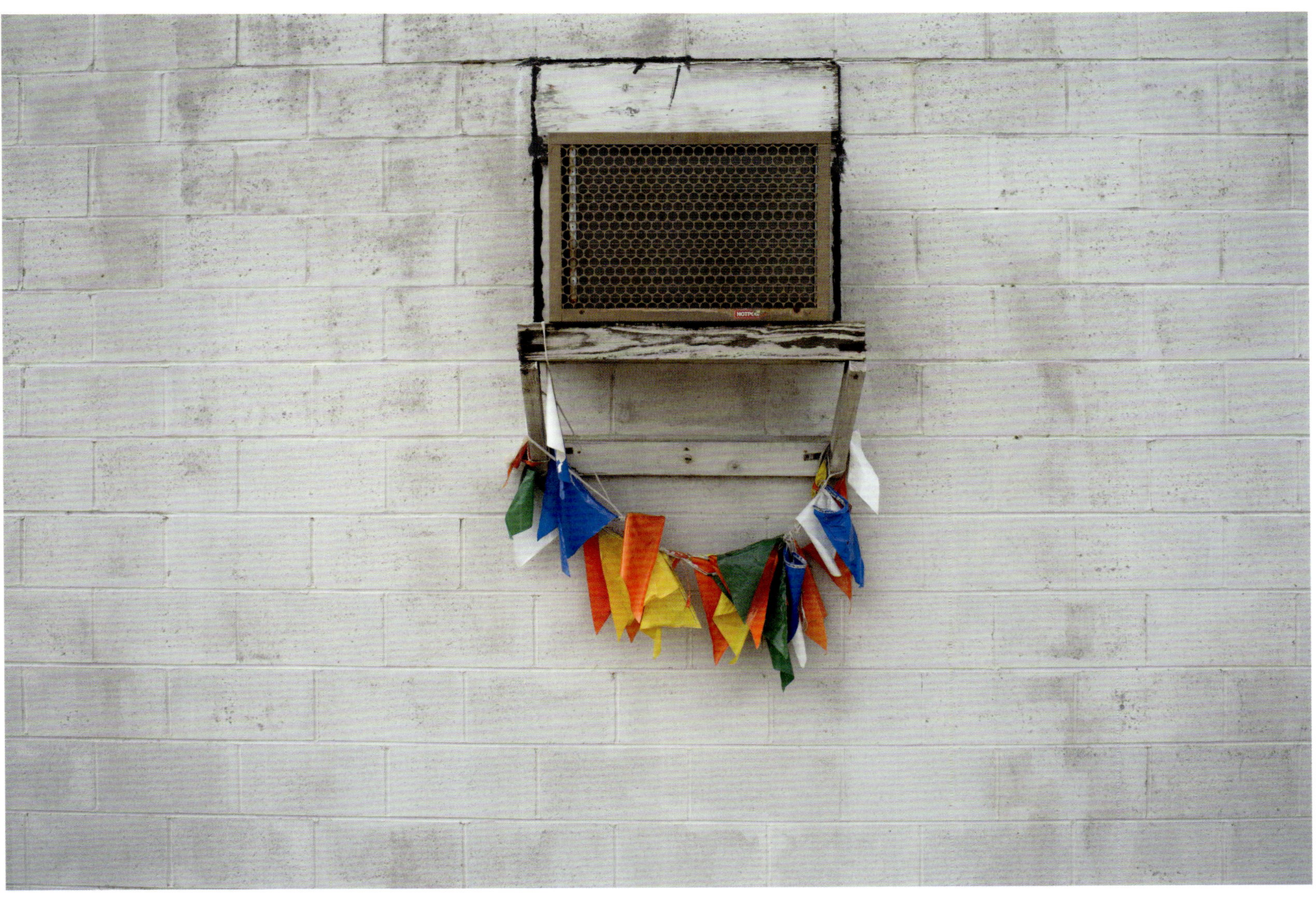

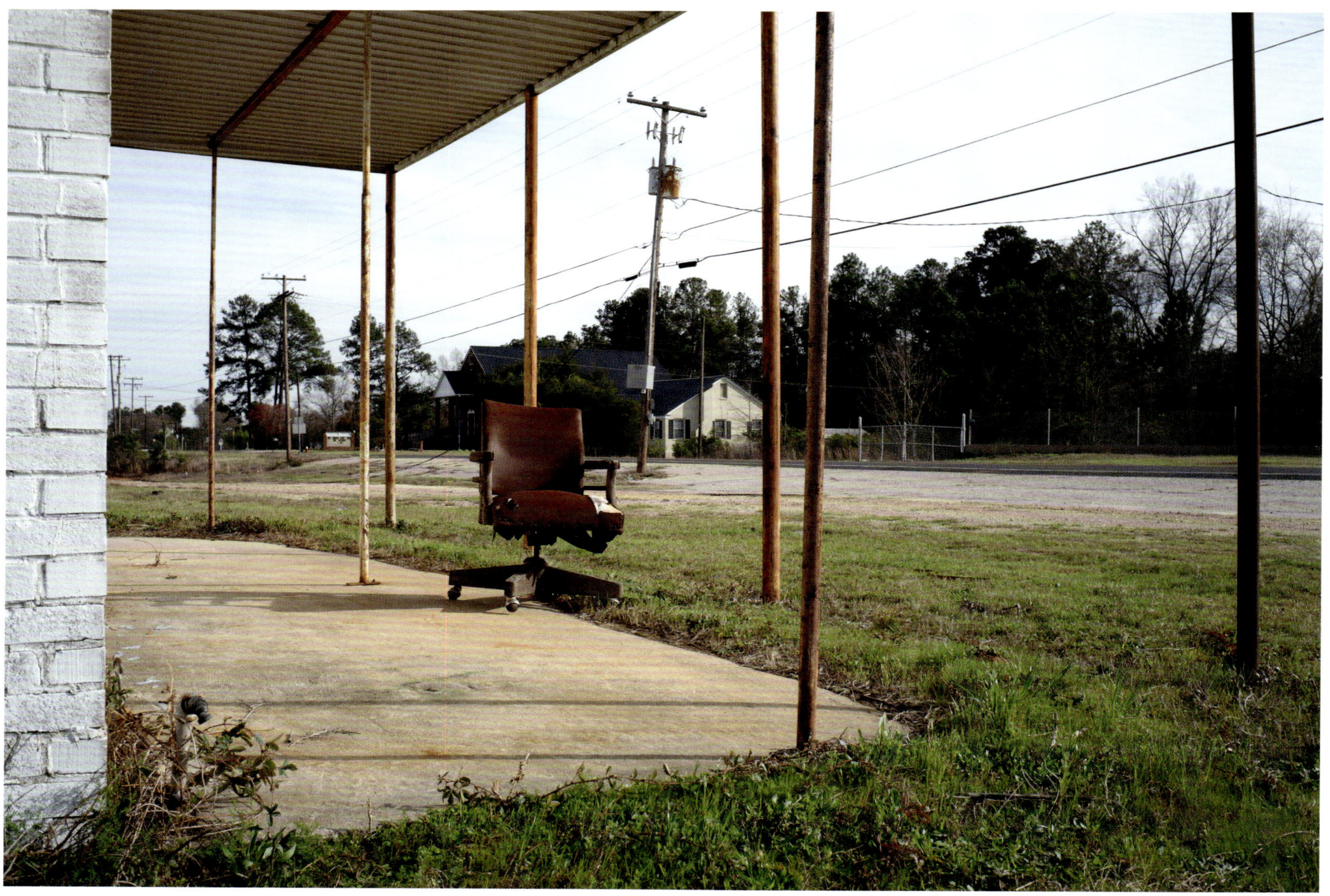

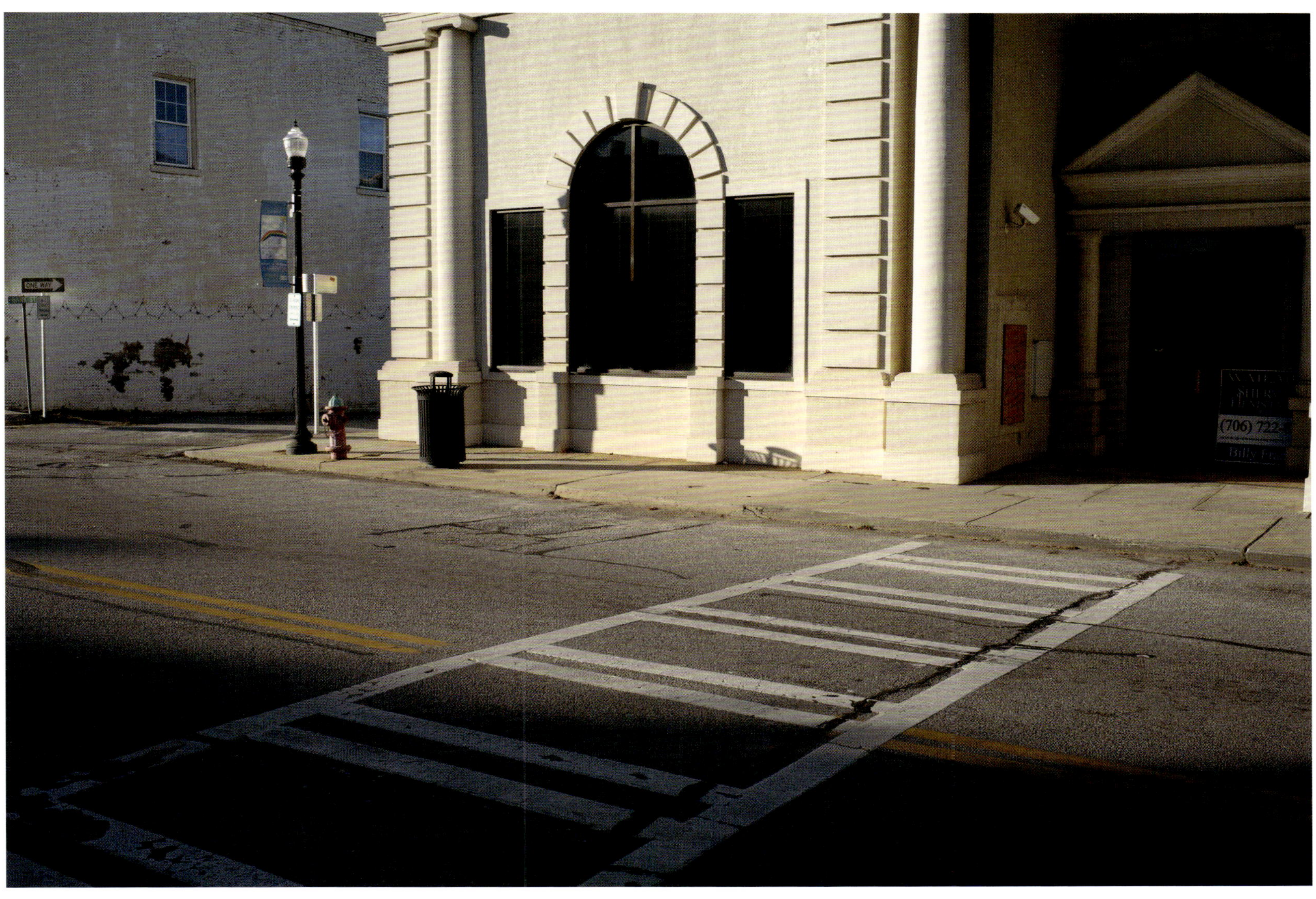

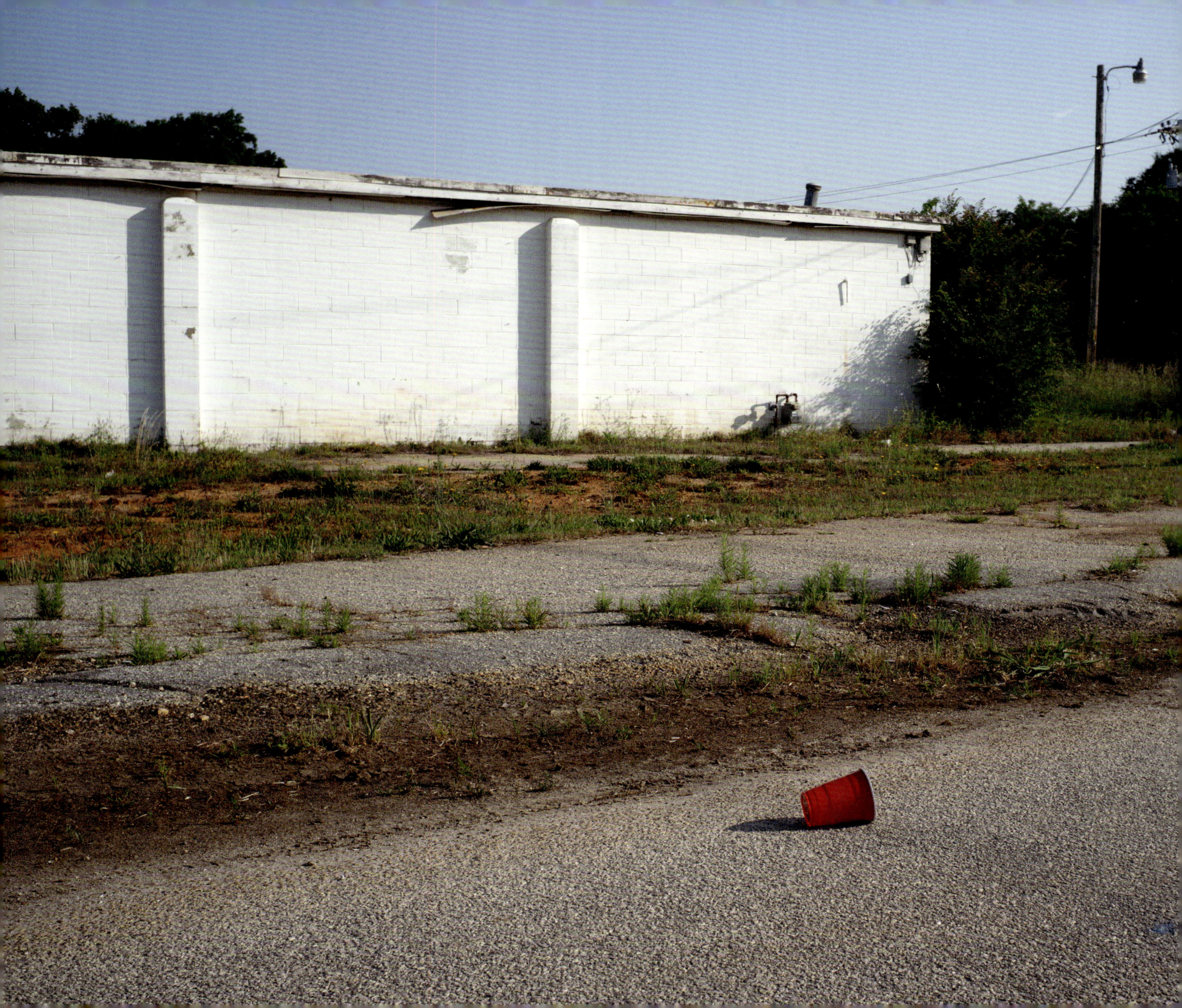

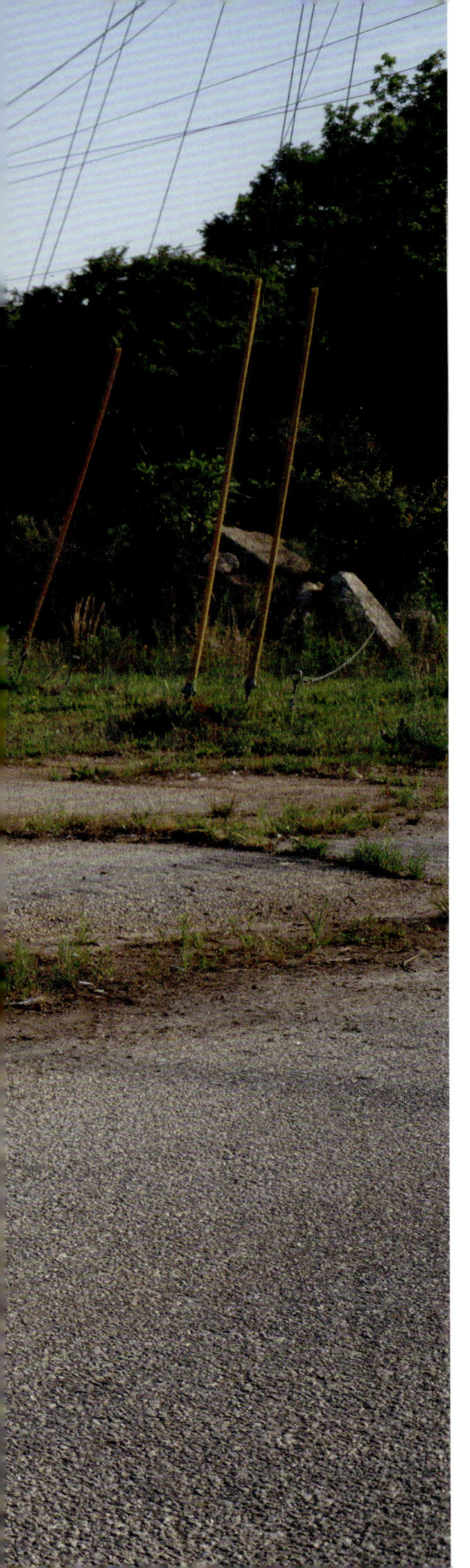

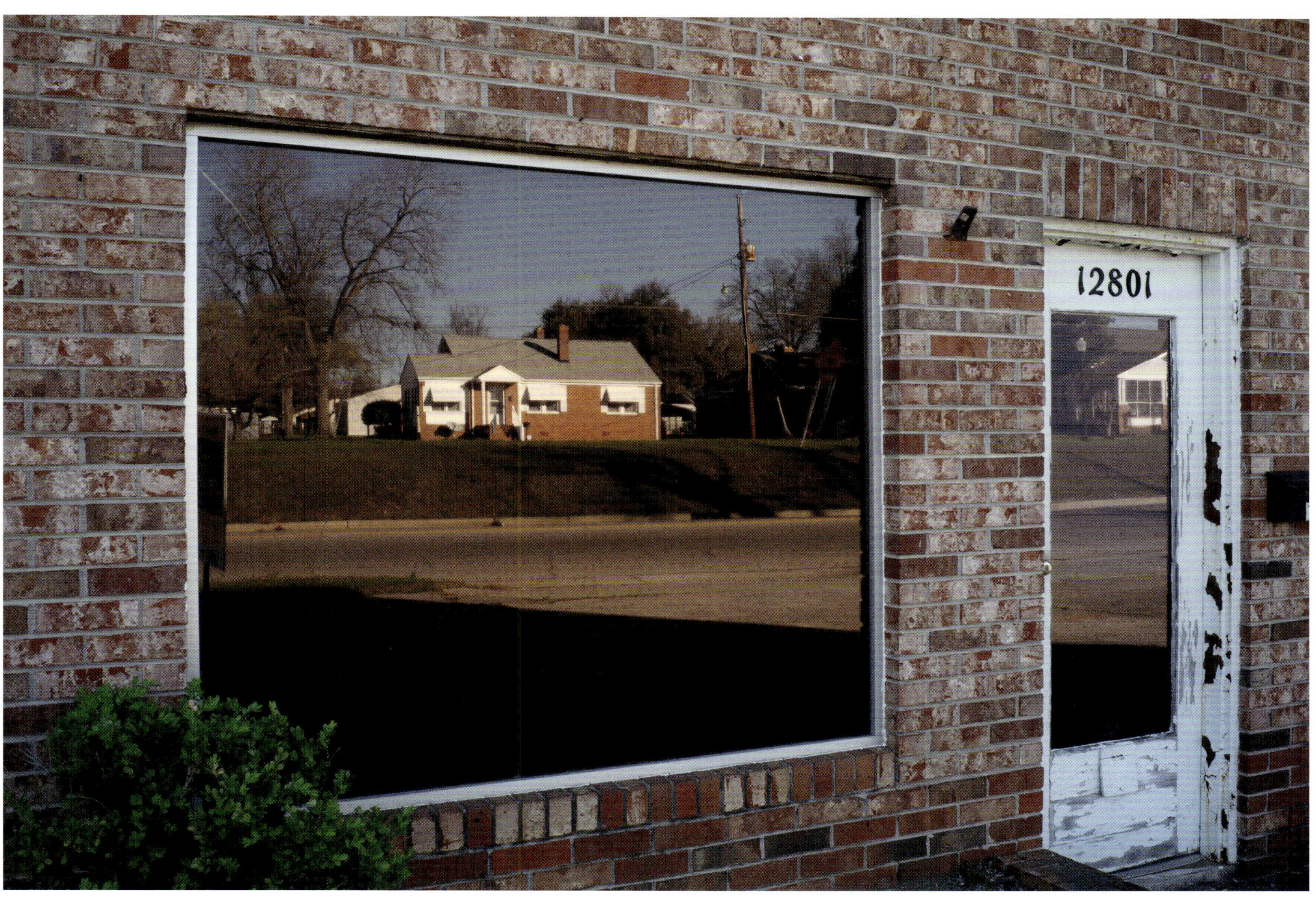
12801

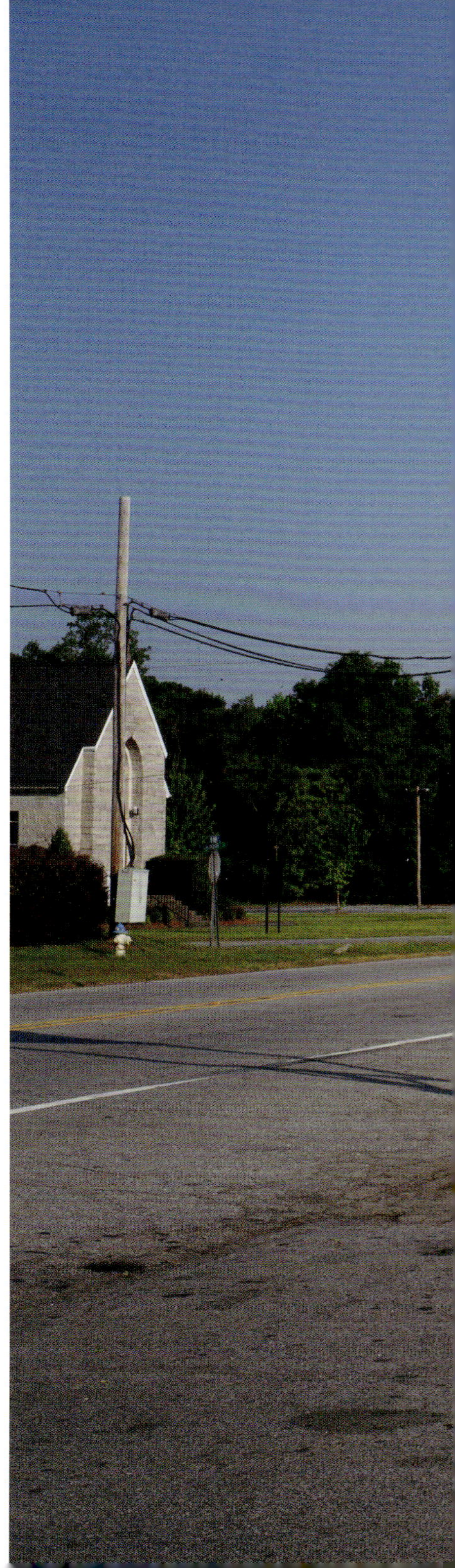

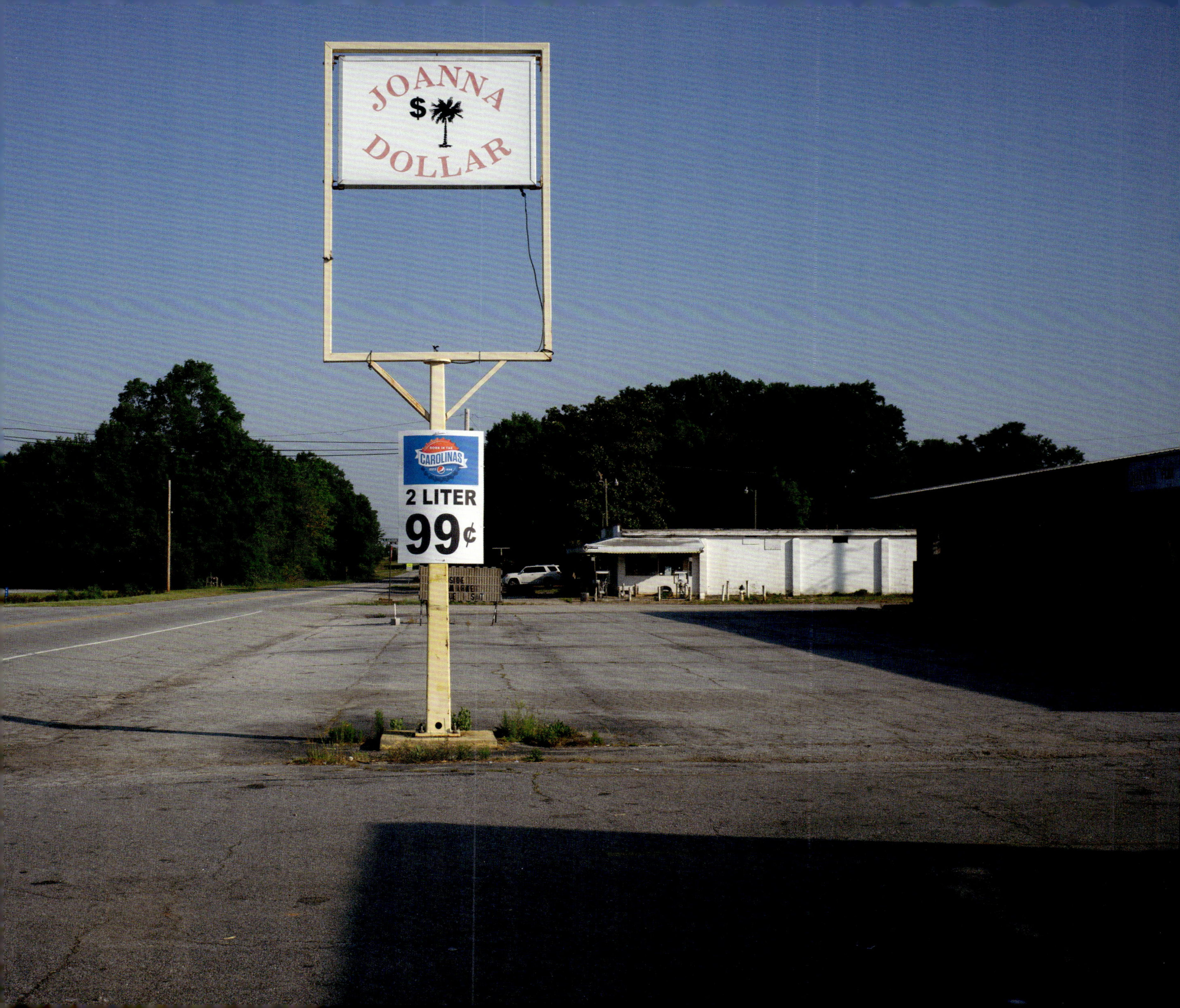

JOANNA
$
DOLLAR
CAROLINAS
2 LITER
99¢

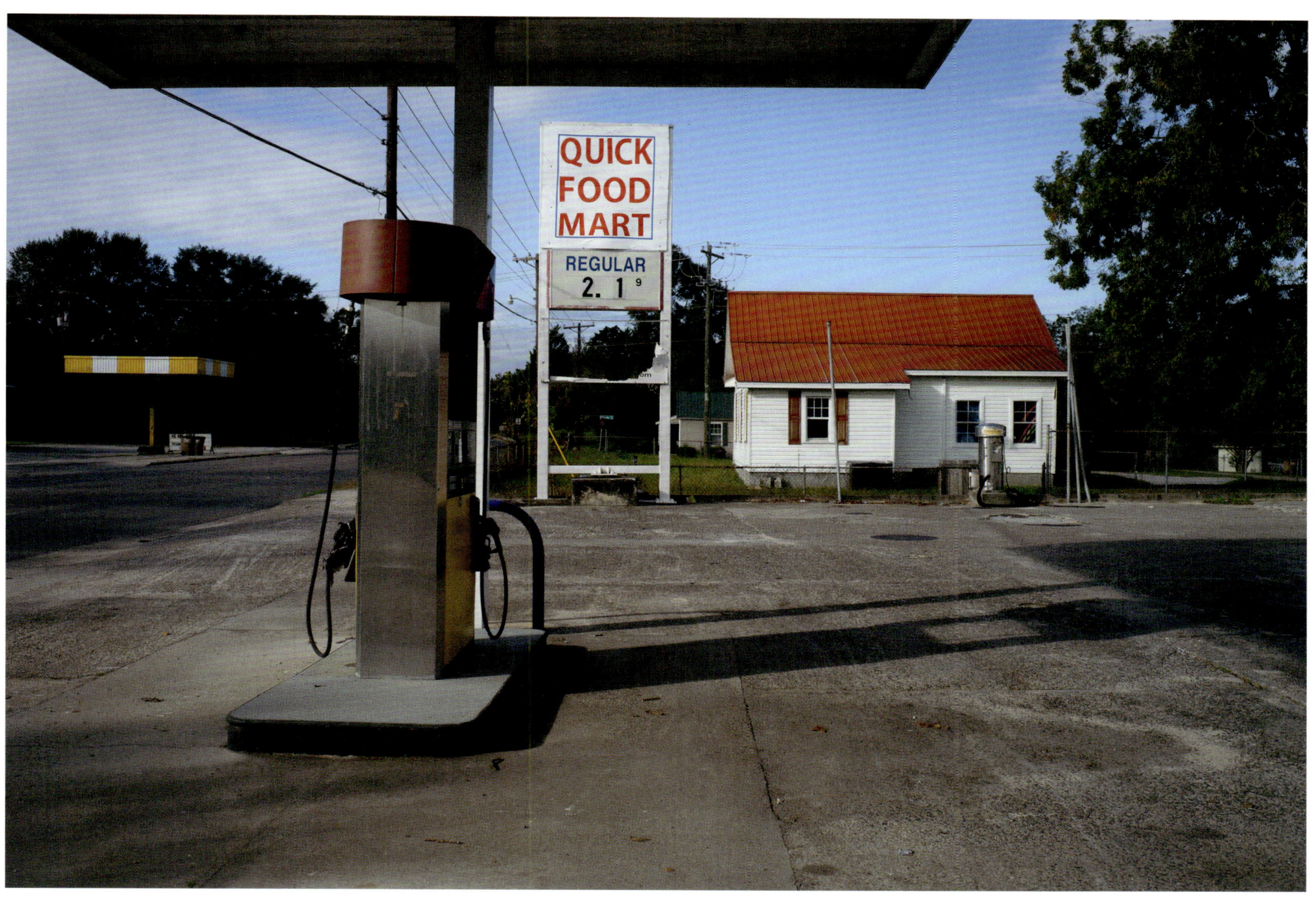
QUICK
FOOD
MART
REGULAR
2. 1 9

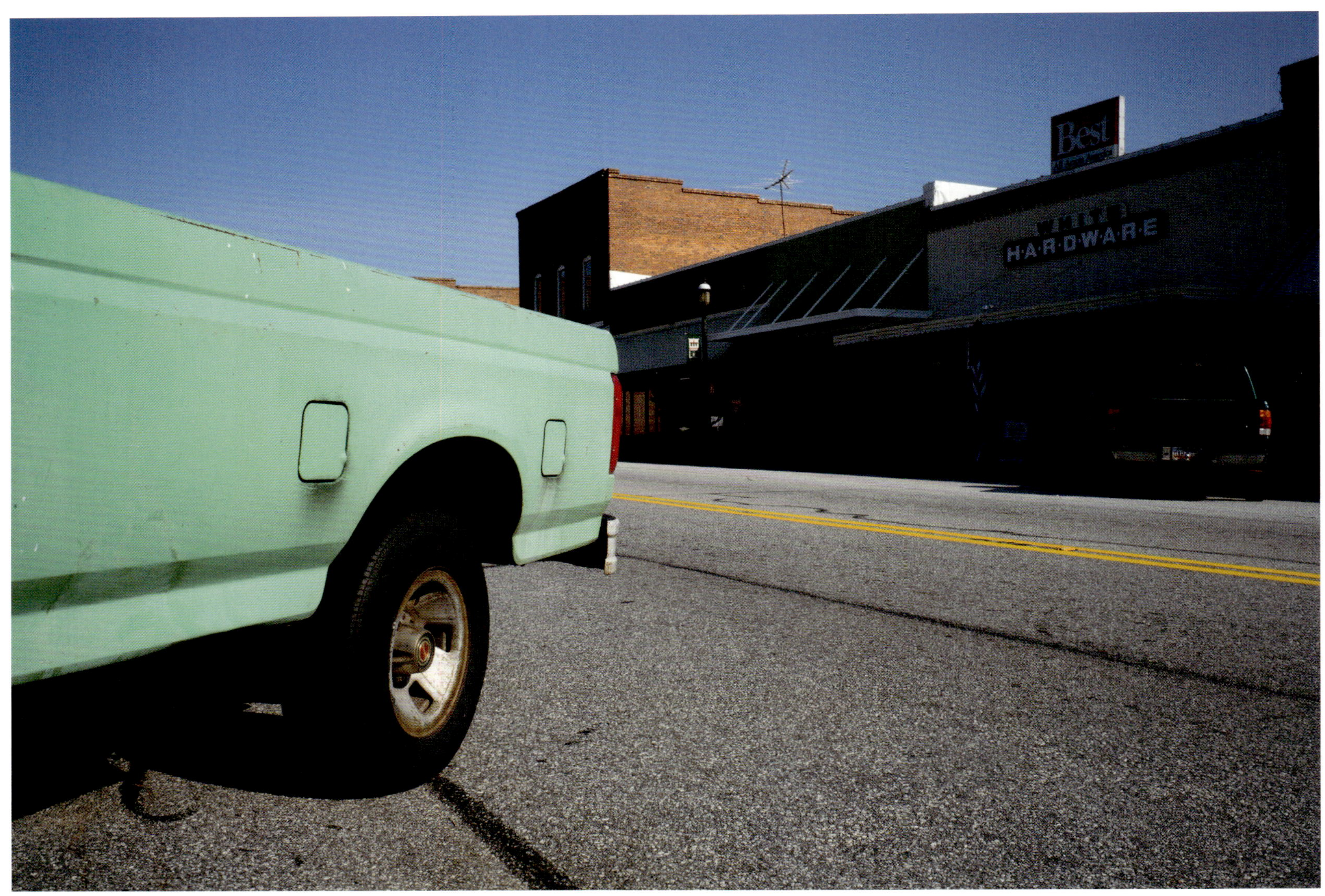
Best
H·A·R·D·W·A·R·E

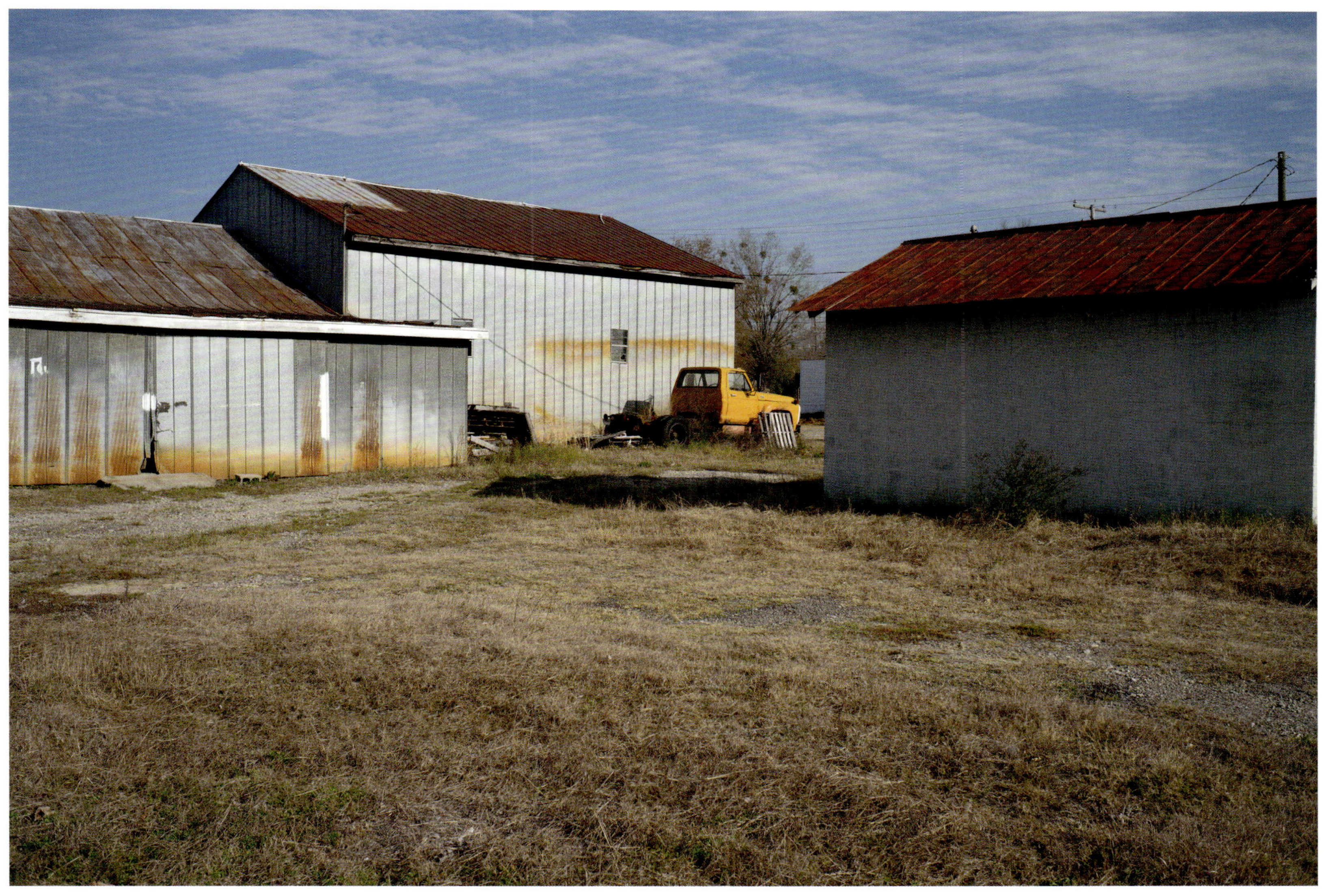

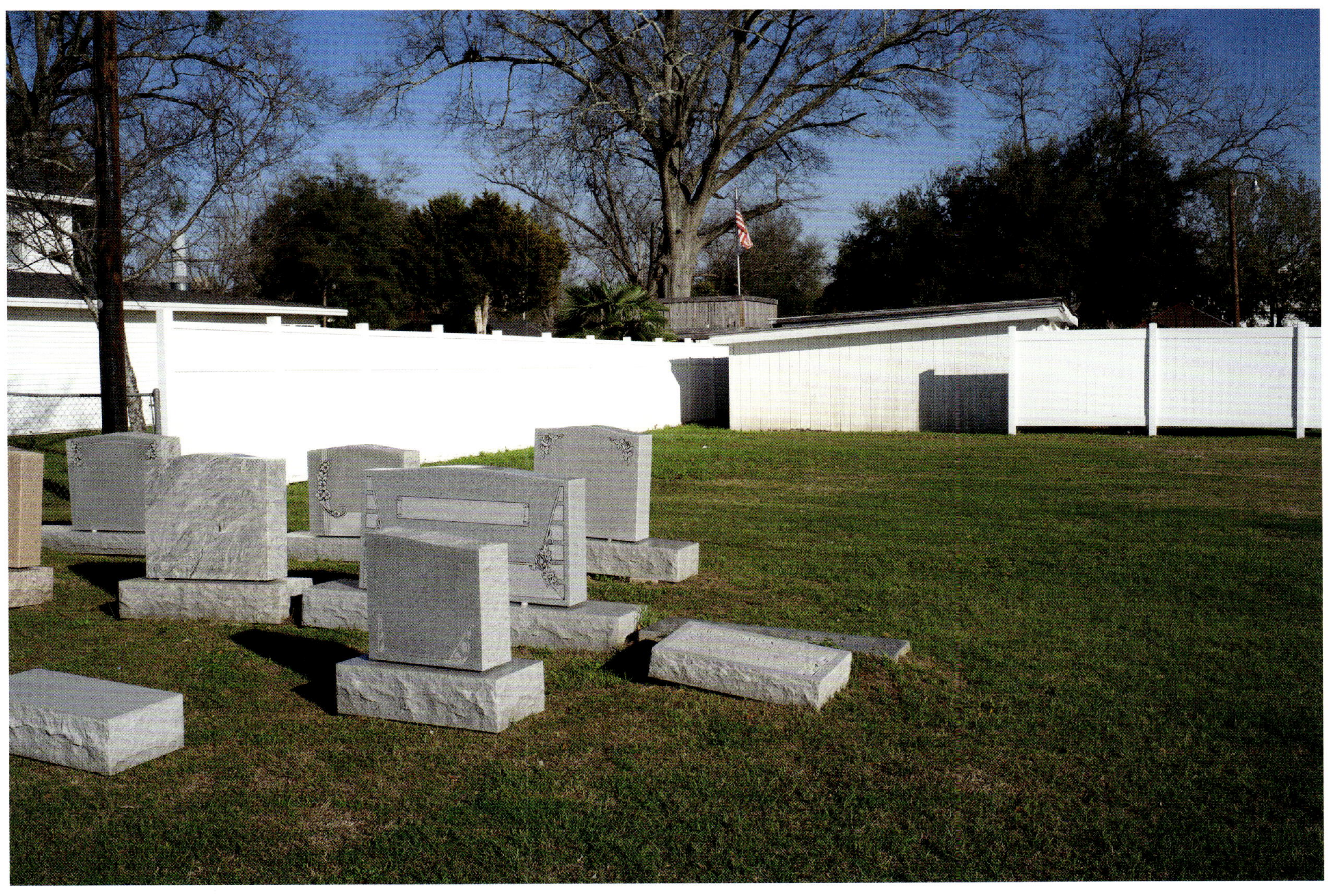

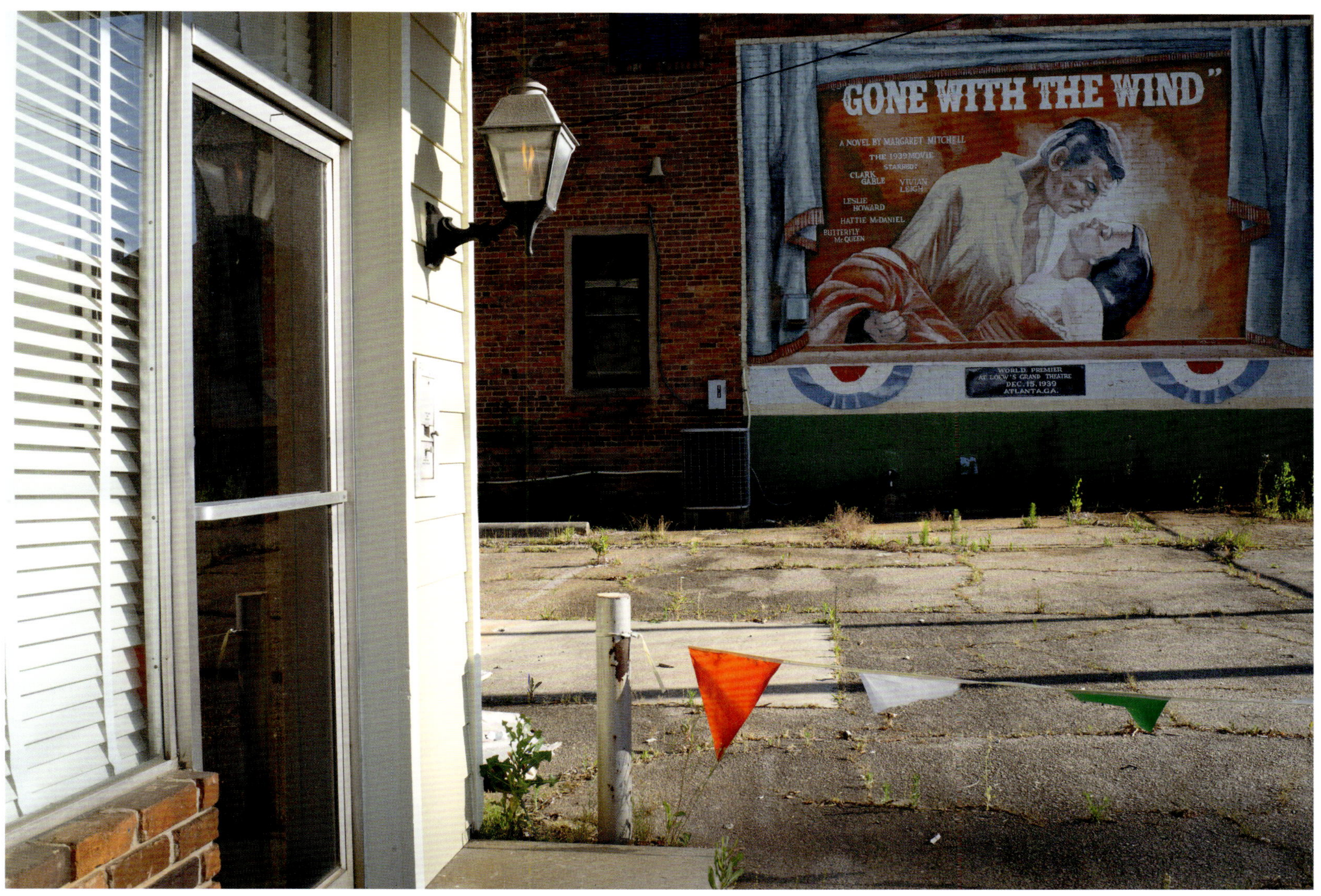
GONE WITH THE WIND"
A NOVEL BY MARGARET MITCHELL
THE 1939 MOVIE STARRED:
CLARK GABLE
VIVIAN LEIGH
LESLIE HOWARD
HATTIE McDANIEL
BUTTERFLY McQUEEN
WORLD PREMIER
AT LOEW'S GRAND THEATRE
DEC. 15, 1939
ATLANTA, GA.

PLATELIST

ACKNOWLEDGMENTS

The greatest of thanks goes to my family:

To my wife, Cristy, for putting up with the ups and downs of everything. I Love You, always, forever, everything, and all of it. You helped push me when no one else could.

To my parents, Cab and Kathy, thank you for your unending support. You put up with a lot, but I wouldn't be who I am without your love and understanding through the good and the bad.

To my late grandfather, L.L., I know you'll never get to read this or see this work physically, but you helped make all of this happen. Without you, I never would have truly appreciated this landscape and found love for the place I was raised. You have been with me in spirit from day one of this project. I'm eternally grateful.

Many thanks, also, to a list of specific people and groups who have been there when I needed them, whether they know it or not:

Matt Porter, The Morris Museum of Art, Jim Stiff, Neal Rantoul, Steve Bliss, Thomas Webster, Leonard "Porkchop" Zimmerman, Jason Craig, Randy Pace, Pax Barrow, Martine Fougeron, Elisabeth Biondi, Lyle Rexer, all at The Photography Master Retreat, my friends at Metro Coffeehouse, and anyone who happened to sit and talk with me about this project over the past few years.

I'm sure some people might have been left out, but know that I appreciate you all the same.

Lastly, I want to thank the people of every town I set foot in while shooting for this work. Thank you for letting me explore your home. I hope that I was able to portray it respectfully and honestly.